LEISA ANSLINGER AND
VICTORIA SHEPP

FORMING
GENEROUS
hearts

STEWARDSHIP PLANNING FOR
LIFELONG FAITH FORMATION

TWENTY
THIRD 23rd
PUBLICATIONS
www.23rdpublications.com

Twenty-Third Publications
A Division of Bayard
One Montauk Avenue, Suite 200
New London, CT 06320
(860) 437-3012 or (800) 321-0411
www.23rdpublications.com

ISBN 978-1-58595-642-5
Library of Congress Catalog Card Number: 2007930536
Printed in the U.S.A.

Contents

Acknowledgments

Our deep gratitude must be expressed to Bill Huebsch, for his guidance and insight. His willingness to collaborate on this project was invaluable, a sign for us of a spirit of ministry to which we aspire.

We also want to acknowledge the contributions of Father Jan Kevin Schmidt and the people of Immaculate Heart of Mary Parish in Cincinnati, Ohio. Their witness to what is possible in the life of the Catholic parish gives us great hope. Many thanks to Msgr. Bill Hanson and the people of St. Gerard Majella Parish in Port Jefferson Station, New York, for their willingness to share their growth as they have embraced engagement and strengths development. Their experience is an encouraging example of pastoral practice. Both these parishes stand as inspiring testimony to the power of the principles offered in this book.

Finally, many thanks to Dr. Al Winseman, Joe Cavanaugh, Cinda Hicks, and the folks at the Gallup Organization. Their study, insight, and commitment offer the potential for lasting change in the Church in the United States, and we appreciate their personal passion for equipping pastoral leaders.

Foreword

Did you ever wonder what would happen in your parish if you combined the power of lifelong faith formation with the parish stewardship program? The results could be spectacular! You're holding the book in your hands that finally makes these connections.

LIFELONG FAITH FORMATION

When you get into the swing of providing people with opportunities for deeper communication with Christ, followed by ways to sustain the excitement of that faith, amazing things happen!

+ People who are "in Christ" are aware of the Spirit within and among them. A strong sense of well-being and gratitude emerges. They experience forgiveness and desire the common good.

+ Such people are more willing to give themselves for the needs of God's work, to feed the hungry and visit the sick, but also to be on committees and assist with parish needs.

+ They're more eager to celebrate excellent liturgies, singing with full voices!

+ They're more ready to open their hearts to strangers, to the rejected, and even to those whom the church does not always welcome fully.

+ And, of course, such folks are also more generous financially, not only to the parish, but also to the hurting and poor.

And aren't those really the goals of any stewardship program?

Forming Generous Hearts

In this marvelous and definitive guide to planning for stewardship in your parish, two authors combine their powerful ministry talents to provide a roadmap for parish success in stewardship, based on the principles of lifelong faith formation. Leisa Anslinger and Vikki Shepp both have long years of dedicated service and both are excellent teachers.

As you move through the chapters of the book, their ability to teach becomes clear. You will realize as you go that "Yes, indeed, I can do this!" They help you see the vision and also the practical steps to implement it. And I'm not kidding, the principles they lay out in this book will change forever the way you approach stewardship in your parish! Those principles are clear, but more than that, they finally help us see that stewardship and lifelong faith formation have the same goals and, in a way, are very related activities! One feeds the other.

Enjoy this book. It's a welcome contribution to the literature of both stewardship and lifelong faith formation.

Bill Huebsch
Pine City, Minnesota

Introduction

What do you most hope and pray for when you think about your parish? Do you wish parishioners were more committed to Christ? Do you hope for more involvement in the parish, or more lively work in service and mission? In the words of one pastor, "I pray that my parishioners will live their faith with the whole of who they are, at the parish, but just as importantly, in their lives. I want the parish to be a place that helps them to be all they are called to be as Christian disciples. I wouldn't be disappointed if, in the midst of that transformation, the parish's bills got paid! In my 'ideal parish,' we would be able to serve those in need in our community and world through living stewardship. People would simply give from their hearts." Now there's a statement of hope for our parishes and our Church! What would happen in the lives of people and in our world if our parishes were more like the one this pastor hopes for?

TWO CONTRASTING EXPERIENCES

Two friends from different parts of the country were chatting about this on Good Friday. One friend said, "Oh, we had the worst Holy Thursday ever. The preaching was irrelevant, the liturgy had distractions, and the assembly was non-responsive. It saddens me that this once vibrant parish is sinking into some sort of apathy and funk. I just might have to find another place to go." The other friend replied, "I'm so sorry to hear that. My parish was like that once, and I was struck last night by how much has changed. The liturgy last night was a true celebration of a thankful community, a gathering of people who are living what they pray. Not only was the liturgy prepared and celebrated well; people truly participate now, and as I watched families arriving, I realized that many of them, most really, are truly living their faith. It took some time to make the changes and it took patience as things developed, but it has been worth it. I wish more people could experience what I did last night."

WHY THIS BOOK NOW?

After hearing and living countless stories like the one above, it became clear that the Church needs more parishes like the second example. We became convinced of the need to equip parishes to become places of living discipleship and stewardship, communities of faith like the one described in the Acts of the Apostles, in which the people possessed "glad and generous hearts" (Acts 2:46). We know there are parishes throughout the United States where people are not just coming to Mass but are fully engaged in the life of the parish. We also know that there are plenty of parishes where this is not the case; ones where attendance, participation, and collections are down; ones that seem to have lost the flame of faith and the fire of love.

So we set out to write a book that provides principles to guide pastoral leaders as they seek to transform their parish into a place where people embrace Christian discipleship. The principles are rooted in the wisdom of our Church's documents, are drawn from exciting work by the Gallup Organization, and reflect pastoral experience, our own and that of many pastoral leaders from parishes throughout the United States. Through our study and experience, we believe we have something to say about the connections between conversion, discipleship, and stewardship, and the ways parishes can foster real life in Christ so that people express their faith through a generous outpouring of love. More importantly, we give you not just the mind stuff (why to do it) but the heart stuff (how it is driven by God) and the hands stuff (how to do it). So, here you have it, a guide to forming generous hearts.

THE STATE OF CATHOLIC STEWARDSHIP

Early in U.S. Catholic history, contributions were low primarily because of the socio-economic status of Catholics. In spite of the limited income, however, the Church was instrumental in the establishment of schools and hospitals, of libraries and social service agencies; Catholics contributed a large portion of their limited income to build churches as lasting testimonies to their faith, serving parishes and neighborhoods for subsequent generations.

As Catholics moved up the socio-economic ladder, however, their giving stayed on the lower rungs. It is well documented that Catholics currently give less than their Protestant counterparts. And this is not due to the clergy abuse scandal: "Per capita monetary giving to Catholic activities is now only half of what it was two decades ago, down from 2.2 percent of income in the early 1960s to 1.1 percent by 1984" (Dorothy Vidulich, "Stewardship also requires greenbacks, critic says," *National Catholic Reporter*, January 8, 1993). Note that the above statement was written well before the publicity of the scandal. After 2002, there wasn't a drop in collections, but a shift in the type of donating: "Catholics put an estimated $5.8 billion in Sunday collection baskets to support their local parishes in 2002, an increase of 4.9 percent, or twice the rate of inflation. Yet they cut their pledges to bishops' annual appeals for diocesan operations by 2.3 percent, to $635 million" (Alan Cooperman, "Catholic donations rise, despite sex scandal," *Washington Post*, November 7, 2003). Additionally, there have been more contributions to foundations and creative financing.

The church does have wealth—real estate, financial assets, and the like. However, there are some common misconceptions about the Church's wealth and finances according to Charles Zech: "In spite of its enormous wealth, the U.S. Catholic church faces many challenges in meeting its responsibilities. These responsibilities involve supporting a variety of ministries, including worship, teaching, evangelization, service, and developing Christian community" ("Population shifts pose problems, opportunities for church finance," *National Catholic Reporter*, August 12, 2005). These misconceptions may be part of the reason some Catholics don't give. Dorothy Vidulich reported that "Hartford Auxiliary Bishop Peter A. Rosazza said many financial problems the church faces are 'unknown to average Catholics.' If they were actively involved, they would contribute more" ("Stewardship also requires greenbacks, critic says," (*National Catholic Reporter*, January 8, 1993).

A NEW LENS

Now, fifteen years later, we know that Bishop Rosazza was on to something. When people are engaged in their parish, they are not only better stewards of money, they contribute to the creation of a dynamic parish and their faith influences the way they live their lives. As Patricia Lefevere, writing about researcher-psychologist Paul Baard, reports in the *National Catholic Reporter*, "The degree that churches meet basic motivational needs, people attend more frequently, give at higher levels, offer their services more often, and even in some cases go on to full-time ministries" ("Church grows when pastor helps people find God's love," *National Catholic Reporter*, December 21, 2001).

Groundbreaking work by Dr. Al Winseman and the Gallup Organization provides a clearer understanding of the connection between parishioner engagement (which we will explain in more detail as we explore the first principle for parish life) and spiritually committed individuals—people who give generously of themselves in service to their parish and neighborhoods and who contribute financially to a much greater degree than their "not-engaged" counterparts. Grasping this research and reflecting on it in relationship to our parishes will cause us to shift our focus in some crucial ways. The studies, particularly when considered side-by-side with the vision of the gospels, New Testament accounts of the early Church, and current Church documents, provide a lens through which to take a new look at what we do in parish life, and why.

This book is for pastors, parish leadership teams, parishioner leaders or pastoral staffs, parish pastoral council members, stewardship commission or committee members, faith formation committees or planning groups, spiritual life or worship committees or guiding groups, finance or administration commission or committee members, long-range planning teams, and anyone interested in contributing to the life of your parish. The process it supports will be most effective if you read it together, using the book as a journal, workbook, and planning tool. Each section includes questions for your personal reflection as well as suggestions for discussion among your group(s). Set aside time to discuss each principle and additional time after you have studied all that is included in the pages that follow.

This book is divided into seven sections, each devoted to a principle for parish life. At the end of the book there is a planning process to help shape your parish's life based on the principles, plus a list of helpful resources and Web sites where you can acquire additional learning and support.

The **Seven Principles for Parish Life** will lead to embracing a life of discipleship and stewardship, as individuals and as a community of believers. The principles are born of pastoral leadership experience in parish and diocesan ministry, through careful study of sacred scripture, theology, Church documents, current research, and in conversation with friends and colleagues throughout the United States. The principles are all interrelated; together they provide direction for you as a pastoral leader as you guide your parish to live faithfully as disciples and stewards. Within the Principles sections, we will define terms used by people of ministry in a variety of disciplines, to support dialogue among leaders in all aspects of the life of your parish. We will point out topics that are explored further on our Web site (www.thegenerousheart.com) and resources for your consideration as you develop strategies based on your study and discussion of the seven principles.

Within these principles, the background for **Developing a Vision** is included. By carefully reading sacred scripture and our Church's documents, a vision of the Christian community as lived out in the Catholic parish begins to emerge. In the introduction to their pastoral letter on adult faith formation, the U.S. bishops tell us that adopting practices that contribute to this vision sets the stage for a community of people who possess a "lively baptismal and eucharistic spirituality with a powerful sense of mission and apostolate" (*Our Hearts Were Burning Within Us*, USCCB: Washington, 1999), and are therefore ready to step out in faith. Following a scriptural piece that keeps us connected to the ministry of Jesus and the early Church, the vision sections of this book will put you in touch with insights from our Church's documents in relationship to our seven principles.

After developing a vision, we examine and **Explore Successful Practices**. Embracing the vision of each principle leads us to develop corresponding practices for our parish communities. Therefore each chapter includes successful practices used by parishes as they step out in faith. Sometimes it is helpful to learn from the experiences of others who share a common vision. The practices are provided as a way of "priming the pump" for the development of your own practices.

Lastly, the book concludes with a process dedicated to **Shaping Parish Life**. Once you have acquired or developed your understanding of this vision of the parish as a community of disciples and stewards, you will be eager to help your parish begin or continue to embrace the principles found within this book.

The only way to affect growth or to develop strategies that will benefit your parish and its members is to take the vision that you will acquire here and let it guide you as you put a plan into place. You can read this book knowing you are being equipped to lead your parish to become a community of discipleship and stewardship.

FORM A GENEROUS HEARTS TEAM

It will be most helpful to have a group of people in your parish read this book at the same time, study the principles and vision, and consider your current practices. Look at your parish and build your Generous Hearts Team to reflect the people who are part of it: youth; young adults (single and married); adults (single and married); older adults; ethnic and cultural groups (those currently represented and those who are in the pews but may not be involved); male and female. In other words, include everyone! Then, your team will be ready to consider your community's needs and the hopes you have for your parish through the Shaping Parish Life process.

PARISHES COME IN ALL SHAPES AND SIZES

Every parish has its own distinct rhythm, with elements that constitute life within the faith community for its parishioners. Many Catholic parishes today find the composition of the parish or its leadership changing:

+ declining neighborhoods often result in dwindling membership;

+ parishes that were once homogeneous in cultural composition are now rich with ethnic diversity;

+ parishes are clustered together for purposes of planning and administration, often with a canonical pastor and one or more pastoral administrators or parish life coordinators;

✛ suburban parishes are often large and complex;

✛ some parishes have Catholic schools that are thriving; for others, once-vibrant schools now face declining enrollment, closure, or the formation of a regional school system.

Every parish has its particular character with its corresponding challenges. Our hope is that, as you read this book and discuss its contents with your Generous Hearts Team and others, you will take the character of your parish into honest account. The principles and vision explored within this book will remain constant, but the way in which life is shaped based upon the principles is certain to be different for every parish.

Now, before you proceed, consider your own parish. No one needs to know your assessment, unless you decide to share it. Or, invite your Generous Hearts Team to discuss these questions with you as you begin to dream about your parish's future.

✛ What evidence do you have that parishioners embrace a living relationship with Christ that leads them to be people of profound generosity, who live their faith with the hands of a servant?

✛ What are the special challenges that your parish faces at this time? How can you construct your Generous Hearts Team in a manner that will insure thorough representation, so that the conversations that take place will take the character of your parish into honest account?

✛ How is each member encouraged to grow in faith throughout his or her lifetime?

✛ How is your parish, and how are your parishioners, embracing a life of generous stewardship of all you are and have and will be?

✛ In what ways does your community care for those most in need? How do parishioners live their faith in their lives away from the parish, in their homes, places of work, and in the world?

We are the two friends whose Holy Thursday story began this introduction. Our experience is yours, we are sure; our story is your story. We, like you, know that our parishes can be places of hope and love, signs of Christ's loving presence in our lives and in our world. We need only look again at all we are and do within parish ministry, consider the principles in this book, draw others to share this common vision of parish life with us, and take some first steps to make the vision a reality. Our parishes (and we ourselves) will be transformed, as we become communities of disciples and stewards who live their faith with glad and generous hearts.

PRINCIPLE I

Belonging

"Teacher," he said, "What must I do to inherit eternal life?"

He said to him, "What is written in the law? What do you read there?"

He answered, "You shall love the Lord your God with all your heart, and with all your soul, and with all your strength, and with all your mind; and your neighbor as yourself."

He said to him, "You have given the right answer; do this, and you will live." ~LUKE 10:25–27

Foster a sense of *belonging* among all who come to the parish, and develop that sense of belonging among members throughout the moments of their lives and stages of their faith. This is the first principle.

At a recent parish leadership gathering, a parishioner shared how important belonging to the faith community has been for him and his wife. Mark explained

For a long time, my wife and I came to Mass here, but we were not deeply involved in the parish community. My wife went to a Bible study at a local Christian church with her women friends from our neighborhood. We even did *Purpose Driven Life* with the same group. It was hard coming to Mass but not really feeling a part of the community. While we appreciated what we were learning about God's word with our Protestant friends, there was nothing about the sacraments, nothing about the richness of our Catholic tradition. We were torn; we loved our friends, but we sensed we were missing something in our lives. Through God's grace my wife was moved to experience a parish retreat here, and she met a group of women whose company she really enjoyed. Slowly she became connected here. God's hand continued at work in this; she and I joined the other women and their husbands to form a small faith community and the friendships that developed in that group have changed our lives. As I look back, I think God thought I really needed intense support. Three of the strong Christian men in our group are now in formation for the diaconate (and continue to guide and inspire me)! It was, and is, belonging to this group of Catholic people that has brought me into the life of the parish and has made me a stronger Christian.

The conversation that followed Mark's sharing was deeply moving. At round tables, each parishioner told a little of his or her own story. One by one, the participants expressed gratitude that someone had taken time to invite and encourage their involvement and deepening relationship with the faith community. For each person in the room, that initial relationship with the community had resulted in a more profound relationship with Christ; God became more "real" and connected to their every day lives through the reality of parish life.

BELONGING AND BELIEF

What unfolded in this discussion illustrates findings in recent Gallup Organization studies. In most cases, belief does not lead to belonging, but rather, belonging leads to belief (Albert L. Winseman, *Growing an Engaged Church*, Gallup Press, New York, 2007, p. 44). The Christian community is the embodiment of the Body of Christ. As such, we experience Christ's presence through one another, particularly when we gather at the Eucharistic table. It stands to reason, then, that the parish community should be one that has its arms wide open at all times for every person. Fostering a sense of belonging is vital, since this

---

Engagement is a sense of belonging.

Engaged parishioners:

- » are loyal and have a strong psychological connection to their parish;
- » are more spiritually committed;
- » are more likely to invite friends, family members, and coworkers to a parish event;
- » give more, both financially and in commitment of their time;
- » organize their lives around their parish because through it their faith has grown and deepened;
- » have found opportunities to serve and help others in their parish;
- » have developed their most meaningful interpersonal relationships in their parish.

(**Growing an Engaged Church**, p. 67-68)

Think of your own experience. When did you move from "going to Mass" to having a sense of *belonging* in your parish? Who or what helped facilitate that movement?

is the way many will experience and deepen their faith in Christ. The most striking element of the Gallup research may be this: parishioner engagement, that sense of belonging to the parish, is primarily a result of *feeling* that we are of value to the community.

CHANGING THE WAY THE PARISH FEELS

The parishes that seem to live discipleship and stewardship most fully are ones in which people say, "when I am there, it feels different than when I am at another church." That feeling comes from people who are spiritually committed individuals. These people know their parish as the place that supports them throughout their lives in Christ; they know that others depend on them to recognize their needs, respond to them, and acknowledge the ways in which each person contributes to the whole. That feeling comes when we are in the presence of a group of people who have fallen in love with Christ and from whom that love flows out. They seek to have the mind of Christ, to set their hearts on all that is holy, and to offer their lives in loving imitation of our self-emptying Lord. Parishes that are communities of this sort are attentive to the many ways in which we may set the stage for building a strong relationship with Christ, and in which people may become engaged in the life of the faith community.

Lives are Changed

Engagement, true belonging, leads people to happier lives. In fact, the people who are engaged are vastly more likely to strongly agree with this statement: "I am completely satisfied with my life" (Winseman, 39). We know that people who take discipleship seriously still experience life's challenges; if anything, disciples know the depth and breadth of all that life holds for them, both

Indicators of a Parish's Spiritual Health

Four Important Outcomes
» Inviting
» Giving
» Serving
» Life
  Satisfaction

challenges and joys. Engagement in the faith community, however, helps to root us in the fullness of hope in Christ, giving our lives more meaning and purpose.

Those who are engaged are also much more likely to *invite* others to join them at a parish function (worship, social, service, or catechetical); they *serve* more in their community, and *give* more of their financial resources to the parish. While in the past, most parishes have spent much energy and attention on developing the actions noted above, the studies show clearly that inviting, serving, giving, and life satisfaction are *outcomes*, and are the result of engagement and spiritual commitment. This information is vital for us as we shape parish practice. We should be attentive to the many ways in which we can build engagement in our parishes, with the assurance that the important outcomes will follow (Winseman, 39–43).

Engagement is key to drawing people toward powerful expressions of faith. In short, true belonging leads to living discipleship and stewardship. There is a caveat here, however. Gallup survey (2001–2005) information indicates that only sixteen percent of Catholics are fully engaged in their parishes; forty-nine percent are not engaged (and just waiting to be drawn more deeply into the faith community, and through the community to Christ); thirty-five percent are actively disengaged (diminishing the community through apathy or negativity).

Two Other Types of Parishioners

The "Not Engaged":
- » may attend regularly, but do not have a strong emotional connection to the parish;
- » are connected socially more than spiritually;
- » give moderately but not sacrificially;
- » do a minimal amount of service in the community;
- » are less likely to invite others and are more likely to leave;
- » are not negative, and are just waiting for an opportunity to become engaged.

The Actively Disengaged Fall into Two Groups:
- » Apathetic:
  - • come only once or twice a year if at all;
  - • can tell someone which parish they belong to, but often by location rather than by name;
- » Physically present but psychologically hostile:
  - • are almost always present,
  - • are unhappy with their parish and insist on sharing their misery with just about everyone.

(**Growing an Engaged Church**, p. 68-70)

THE REAL POSSIBILITIES

This is an area of great concern and of great potential! Think for a moment of all that could happen in the lives of people and in the life of your parish community, not to mention the world, if only a small portion of the currently "not engaged" were to experience true belonging. Rather than exhausting ourselves in trying to meet the demands of the actively disengaged, those who interpret the data suggest strengthening the engaged and focusing our outreach on the "not engaged." A parishioner leader recently commented on this insight.

> This makes sense to me, to concentrate on the "not engaged." I spent ten years of my life teaching and practicing the concept of total quality management, and at the end of it, realized I had spent ten years beating my head against the wall, trying to make everyone happy, rather than focusing my energy and attention on the areas in which I had the greatest possibility of success. We should learn from experiences like that and adjust our practices, in business and in the Church, accordingly.

Keeping the importance of engagement in mind, you can begin to examine your current practices and make subtle shifts, reaching out to those who are with you every week but who do not feel they truly belong. If belonging is as vital as the Gallup research and conversations such as the one with Mark described above demonstrate, there must be things your parish can do to create an atmosphere in which people sense that they truly belong to the community.

BELONGING LEADS TO COMMITMENT

What will you really be trying to do as you foster a sense of belonging in the parish community? That sense of belonging is important because people who have a deep relationship with their faith community are more likely to be spiritually committed. That's the crux of the Gallup Organization's understanding of engagement. Spiritually committed people, people whose faith shapes the way they live, are more likely to exhibit those outcomes we spoke of earlier, of inviting, serving, giving, and life satisfaction. The spiritually committed person has a sense that his or her faith community will support and demonstrate God's love in every moment of life. That is a pretty astounding thing when you think about it! Fostering a sense of belonging helps us to create a place in which people feel at home, a place where we know there is a deep connection between our faith and our life.

DEVELOPING A VISION

> *"Teacher," he said, "What must I do to inherit eternal life?"*
>
> *He said to him, "What is written in the law? What do you read there?"*
>
> *He answered, "You shall love the Lord your God with all your heart, and with all your soul, and with all your strength, and with all your mind; and your neighbor as yourself."*
>
> *He said to him, "You have given the right answer; do this, and you will live." ~LUKE 10:25–27*

This gospel passage was chosen for the beginning of this chapter not because it is the greatest commandment but because of what follows in Luke's account, the parable of the Good Samaritan. This commonly-known parable is often cited as why we should take care of those in need, but we sometimes miss the beginning of the parable in which the lawyer (who had answered correctly, with love of neighbor) continues to question Jesus, saying, "And who is my neighbor?" Jesus didn't simply answer, but instead told the parable of the Good Samaritan to illustrate the concept of neighbor. The *Oxford Bible Commentary* helps us better understand: "Neighborliness knows no bounds and must proceed from an attitude of spontaneity and self-forgetfulness....The parable in its setting calls for an abandonment of all status, privilege, and exclusiveness" (Oxford University Press, 2000, p. 942). When we expand our boundaries and allow for spontaneity, we do abandon our views of who is in or out of the parish and help create that sense of belonging that is vital for engagement. How does your parish answer the question, "who is my neighbor?"

WHAT THE DOCUMENTS SAY

Our Church's guiding documents highlight this need to facilitate belonging. Often, while specifically written for a particular segment of our population, these documents give us a clear understanding of the life we should share with all members. For example, *Renewing the Vision*, the bishops' pastoral letter on youth ministry, provides great insight into creating this sense of belonging. Ministry with youth, it states:

✚ "*reaches* out to young people by meeting them in their various life situations, building relationships, providing healing care and concern, offering a genuine response to their hungers and needs, and inviting them into a relationship with Jesus and the Christian community;

✢ *invites* young people personally into the life and mission of the Catholic community so that they may experience the support, nurture, and care necessary to live as Christians;

✢ *calls* young people to grow in a personal relationship with Jesus Christ, to make his message their own, and to join us in the continuing process of conversion to which the gospel calls us;

✢ *challenges* young people to follow Jesus in a life of discipleship—shaping their lives in the vision, values, and teachings of Jesus and living his mission in their daily lives through witness and service;

✢ *calls young people to be evangelizers* of other young people, their families, and the community" (USCCB, 1997, p. 37).

This development of a sense of belonging is echoed in *Sons and Daughters of the Light* in *Goal Two: Connecting Young Adults with the Church.* There our bishops invite us "to make contact with young adults and to invite and welcome them to participate in the life and mission of the Christian community, which proclaims Jesus Christ by preaching the gospel." The document illustrates this welcome in its first objective: "Evangelizing Outreach: To identify places where young adults gather and to connect them personally with the Church by listening to their concerns, hopes, and dreams, and by welcoming them into a community of faith" (USCCB, 1996, p. 33).

Covering all ages, stages, and ethnicities, *Go and Make Disciples* encourages us with its three goals, particularly the second goal: "To invite all people in the United States, whatever their social or cultural background, to hear the message of salvation in Jesus Christ so they may come to join us in the fullness of the Catholic faith" (p. 57).

EXPLORING SUCCESSFUL PRACTICE

Practice One: Extend a Bigger Welcome

Creating a sense of welcome is not only vital for those who are guests or newcomers, but for every person, at every moment

What vision of a belonging parish emerges for you from these documents? If you were asked to describe this vision in one sentence, what would you say?

of their lives. Talk with people who have been away for a while and have returned. Often, they speak of leaving and wondering if anyone would notice their disappearance, or of being warmly welcomed at another church, and knowing somewhere in their heart that they had found a place where people cared. On their return, if the parish has changed (or they have come back to Catholicism through a different parish), returning Catholics will speak of the importance of being offered a genuine welcome.

When it is genuine (and people will intuitively sense its authenticity), this open-armed and open-hearted welcome is a living manifestation of the Spirit of Christ. Think of the many stories we have of Jesus welcoming people, often those whom the established folks of the time were not thrilled to have in their company: the poor, the widows, children, people who weren't the brightest or the best. Jesus sought out plain people who would become trusted and faithful disciples.

As people come into relationship with Christ through the community, they naturally want to share their love with others, and their welcome is a powerful living extension of the love of God. That is what Mark was describing the night of the parish leaders' meeting. He had a powerful experience of Christ's presence through the people who drew him into the community of believers, just as those who encountered Jesus did when he drew them into the company of those who followed him.

Practice Two: Make Hospitality Your First Rule

Walk into your parish on a Sunday and approach the church as though you were an outsider. Or, visit a parish in which you know no one. What is your first impression? Do you feel that you are valued, that the community that is gathering will be richer for your participation? It seems that many of us spend much time in preparation of the liturgy, which is a necessary and proper thing to do, but we forget that the act of gathering, of coming together for the celebration, begins a long while before the song, Penitential Rite, and opening prayer. The "gathering" really begins in people's hearts, as they gather their thoughts and prepare themselves to pray with the community. The "gathering" begins as parents get young children ready, and as singles, divorced adults, and widows reflect on the week that has passed and ask our Lord to nourish and strengthen them for the week ahead. The "gathering" continues as people park their cars and walk side by side with others with whom they will offer prayers this day. The "gathering" includes the ways in which people are greeted as they arrive in the church building, are assisted if needed as they find a place inside, and look to the people around them for a sign of hospitality.

There are things we can do at church before and after the Mass, too, that will increase the sense of hospitality that people feel upon their arrival. These things could appear to be insignificant, but these small things add up to something much greater. They work together to create an atmosphere of hospitality and warm welcome, as though the Lord himself were standing in our midst (and Christ does stand in our midst, after all!).

Expect Resistance, Invite Inclusion, Multiply Ministry. Sometimes when parish leaders first begin discussing ways to become more hospitable, they encounter unexpected resistance from long-standing members. Much of the resistance has to do with change, and with the uncertainty of what might happen if newcomers offered to become involved. Those who have been stalwart members for years are secure in the knowledge that the parish needs them; what would be the result of welcoming the many new families who arrived for Mass each week?

For example, most parishes already have ushers who faithfully serve each Sunday. Perhaps suggest that the ushers continue to take care of the details inside the worship space. The ushers know how to seat people efficiently, how to take up the collection, assist those with physical disabilities, and help visitors find their family members. The ushers know how to take care of people inside the church, and they are busy with their tasks.

Ministers of hospitality can be recruited for the gathering space and may stand outside, if possible, at least on nice days. These individuals watch for people who need assistance getting into church, warmly greet everyone as they arrive, especially anyone who seems uneasy or unfamiliar, and they distribute the bulletins at the end of Mass. Hospitality ministers outside of the worship space, ushers within. You can double the number of people making certain everyone is taken care of, find new ways for people with the gift of hospitality to serve, and the result will be a new sense of welcome for all who come to be with you for the celebration of the Eucharist. Those who earlier resisted may come to appreciate the increased welcome for liturgies. When that happens, invite them to recruit others to join them. The ministers of hospitality may help with other events at which there will be many visitors, spreading the welcome beyond the Sunday Mass. The solution to the need for better hospitality at Sunday liturgy ripples into other areas of parish life, as long-standing members begin to see the value of the parish they love. They will find that the inclusion of others in ministry enhances the service offered to parishioners, guests, and to those in need in the world.

What about the "person in the pew"? How does the welcome spread beyond those who are designated as ministers of hospitality? Just before Christmas or Easter, many pastors invite their members to extend a special welcome to visitors, "even if they sit in your pew." This always gets a giggle, as many of us find ourselves sitting in the same place week after week. Such a reminder helps not just with the big feasts; once people become aware of the difference a welcome can make, they will find themselves regularly welcoming people, even seeking out guests and newcomers.

Practice Three: Widen the Circles

The situation of already-involved members holding tightly to the ways in which they offer service often extends beyond the celebration of the liturgy. In many parishes, people speak of the 20-80 rule: twenty percent of the people do all the work, while eighty percent attend, benefit from the service of others, and leave. (Remember the principle of engagement: those who are not engaged will not give to the extent of those who are engaged.) The 20-80 rule also applies where financial giving is concerned. In many cases, the same twenty percent who give their time to the parish also give their financial support, while the remaining eighty percent give little if any of their resources. "There's plenty to do around here," you'll hear the twenty percent say, "if others would just step up and offer their help." And yet, many who have offered will point out the ways in which it has been made clear to them that their help is not needed. "I've tried time and again," they'll remark, "but the insiders have it all under control." This inside-outside dynamic is difficult to break through, but it can be done.

A colleague who provides pastoral staff training days encourages people to *"widen the circles."* Picture yourself in church at Mass on Sunday, he'll ask people. Now, look around yourself. Chances are, you know almost everyone who surrounds you, at least by face. You've probably spoken to most of them, and have ministered with many in the last few months. Now, look beyond you. Can you see the faces of the people in the two or three rows just beyond your circle of friends or colleagues? *Widen your circles!* Think about how you might help those people to know their value and to belong. Then, act on what you are thinking about right now. You might be amazed at the result!

Practice Four: Invite People

People in church circles often speak of invitation as being something not very "Catholic," or at the very least something many Catholics are not comfortable with. Even those who want to be inviting often feel inadequate to the task; "I was just never taught to invite people to come to church with me the way my evangelical brothers and sisters were," many will comment. Even when it's a parishioner who could be the object of the invitation, and the invite is simply to a parish event, we may still feel tongue-tied. "What if the person says no?" people wonder. "What if the person agrees, then what?" Yet most of us realize, when we stop to reflect as the parishioner leaders did in our opening story, that an invitation made a remarkable difference in our lives. Most of us become involved, or come to belong more deeply, as the result of an invitation.

So, how to get over invitation-hesitation? This may sound silly, but the first step is to practice! Consider holding an intergenerational catechesis gathering called "How to share your faith with others." The gathering includes time for people to share part of their experience of Christ in their lives, strengthening their own sense of God's presence, and becoming more comfortable in sharing their faith with neighbors, coworkers, or family members. Begin with everyone together, and then invite high school youth to take younger children (with adult leaders) to a separate place for a while. The youth can help the children practice talking with friends and classmates, giving the youth an opportunity to witness as well. Some parishes hold a dry-run practice before phone campaigns to invite members to a special event. No matter how you do it, practicing can be a good step toward becoming more inviting.

Equip people with a card or letter that can be shared with neighbors and friends. Sometimes it is easier to invite someone by giving the person a card that has been prepared by a parishioner team, with the details of the event, including time, location, and a phone number or web address where people can get more details. A pull-out or cut-out section of the bulletin works for this type of invitation as well.

When you focus on "invitation," remember what the outcome is supposed to be: a deep sense of belonging through which people become more deeply conformed to Christ, and in that conformity seek to be more Christ-like.

Practice Five: Focus on New Parishioners

There is no time like the moment when people register in a parish to insure that they are warmly welcomed and invited to become immersed in parish life. Sometimes parish leaders take a new parishioner's desire to join them for granted, or assume that new members will figure out ways to become connected on their own. Yet, the parishes that go out of their way to welcome and provide orientation to new parishioners find that these newest members are often ready and willing to become involved, and will offer meaningful contributions. People who register in our parishes do so because they have sensed that the parish could be a place for them, a place in which they may grow as disciples. These are people who are ready to be drawn deeply into relationship with the community and with Christ. How can you let them know that you are happy that they are coming to be one with you?

While many parishes have some sort of new parishioner welcome ministry, few seem to evaluate what is being done to welcome new members or to think creatively about new possibilities for this ministry. If you're thinking about the importance of belonging and of evangelization as you structure greetings for new parishioners, the ministry that results will be more than one or two moments just after registration. It will more likely be a series of greetings over a period of time that are designed to bring new members fully into the life of the parish.

Many parishes have a team of people who visit the homes of new parishioners, often bringing a small gift or house blessing kit with them. Some have a Bread Ministry, in which the new members are welcomed with a loaf of home-baked bread, along with a note that welcomes them. Following this brief visit with an invitation to a gathering in a parishioner's home or at the parish, many new-parishioner-welcome teams take time to think about ways to invite the new members into a group or ministry that seems particularly appropriate. For example, the mother of an infant might receive a phone call from a member of the Moms' group, or a young adult might be invited to the next parish retreat; a teen might get a phone call from a parish youth who attends the same high school, and an older member who has just moved in with his adult child might be visited by a member of the Knights of Columbus. Becoming acquainted with new members enough to pair them with a person or group with whom they have something in common makes the invitation even more special. What a sign of the way in which the parish values them as a person!

"It's a very exciting time in your life," Debbie remarked on the phone not too long ago. "Let's find a time when we can meet, and I'll walk you through all the steps that will be part of your life in the coming months. You'll see, it will be wonderful!" Debbie is a parishioner who meets with all the couples who are preparing for marriage. She explains the steps of the marriage preparation process, checks in with the couples occasionally to assure them of the parish's prayers and support, and arranges for a parishioner wedding coordinator to facilitate the rehearsal and the wedding celebration. In short, Debbie is a representative of the parish community who warmly welcomes the couple and their family and friends, giving them a gift that cannot be measured. Debbie and the other members of the marriage preparation team let the couples know that the parish is committed to them. The couples come to understand that the parish values them and the sacrament of marriage, and the community rejoices with them in this important moment of their lives.

Sometimes it seems the ways in which our parishes view special moments in people's lives can be a version of "the glass is half-empty," or "the glass is half-full" kind of thinking. Some will say, "I don't know why we bother with so much emphasis on sacramental preparation. People really just want to get it over with, and they don't stick around long afterward. Just give them what they have to have, and move on." Others see sacramental preparation and similar transition moments as opportunities for evangelization, for welcoming people to deepen their relationship with Christ through the community. Sure, there is information to be given to couples preparing for marriage, or for new parents preparing for the baptism of their child. Children need to prepare for their first reception of the sacraments of penance or Holy Communion, and often their parents need to refresh their understanding of these sacraments.

Those moments, however, also have much evangelization potential. A healthy balance between information-giving and relationship-building can do much to help people feel that the parish values them and desires their continued presence within and for the community.

Practice Six: Keep the Door Open

When people have been away from the Church for a while or have been considering Catholicism and are ready to inquire about the catechumenate, it is often tough to make the first phone call or to approach a priest or pastoral staff person. A simple way to invite and facilitate those early conversations is an Open Door session. Open Door typically takes place three times a year, once in the fall, once a couple of weeks after Christmas, and once just after Easter. Have announcements in the bulletin and at the end of Mass. Place posters in the vestibule if possible, or on an outdoor sign. The announcement can read, "There's always an open door here. If you have been away from the church for some time, or would like more information about Catholicism, or if you simply have questions you'd like to ask, a team of caring people will be waiting for you." (Then list the time and location of the meeting.) The gathering is simple, too: a few nice refreshments and the opportunity for each person to introduce himself or herself and explain what brings them there; a few listening people who are familiar with the catechumenate and returning Catholic processes; and time for each person to talk individually with one of the team members. Each person leaves with a good sense of what could come next: updating for someone who has been away for a while; the inquiry for a person who is ready; a meeting with a member of the annulment team for another.

A year ago, a parish held an Open Door session in the midst of the Easter season, and it happened that the announcements were made at Sunday Masses at which First Communion was being celebrated. The following week, a woman called the parish office. "I heard the announcement," she said, "and I felt that Father was talking to me. I have been away from the Church for so long, and was only there on Sunday for my granddaughter's First Communion. I didn't expect to be receiving a gift myself! What a great sign of the way your parish cares for people, no matter who they are or where they are in life."

Fostering a sense of belonging in our parish communities is really about helping people to know the love of Christ through the flesh and blood of real people.

Practice Seven: Do Great Things with Great Care

Be mindful of doing great things with great care, especially the celebration of the liturgy. There is no better way to help people feel they belong than to take the time to gather well, pray well, reflect well, and be sent out with a sense that what we are about when we are together is of great value. What we welcome and invite people into is the life of the Christian disciple, nourished and shaped by our celebrations of the paschal mystery of God's love for us in Christ. In the midst of all that we will discuss, it is important to keep our priorities straight: our primary and central action is the celebration of the Eucharist and our sacramental life. While there are many elements that work together to shape the community of faith, we must not lose sight of what is most fundamental.

Practice Eight: Play Together!

"The parish that plays together stays together," one pastor is fond of saying. Offer people the opportunity to get to know each other through socials, game nights, parents night out events, potluck dinners, picnics, and movie nights. The possibilities are only limited by the imagination of those who plan such events. Draw together a group of hospitality-gifted members and set them loose!

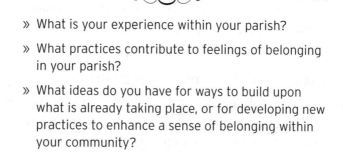

> » What is your experience within your parish?

> » What practices contribute to feelings of belonging in your parish?

> » What ideas do you have for ways to build upon what is already taking place, or for developing new practices to enhance a sense of belonging within your community?

Lifelong Transformation

He brought Simon to Jesus, who looked at him and said,
"You are Simon son of John. You are to be called Cephas,"
which is translated Peter. ~JOHN 1:42

Experience deep conversion to *Christ* and create a climate in which everyone is given the opportunity to encounter and be drawn into life in Christ. This is principle number two.

Jim and Eileen came out of church obviously shaken. Jim struggled to compose himself. Hugging a friend, he said, "I needed that." He explained,

I came into church tonight extremely angry. A young relative, Jeremy, and a friend got into a taxi last night, and on their way, they got into an argument with the taxi driver, an argument about faith in Christ and belief in a loving God. When Jeremy got out of the taxi, the driver ran him over, crushing his legs. Later, the police found the driver. He had stolen the taxi and is now under arrest. Jeremy underwent massive surgery today and his prognosis is still extremely guarded. So, I arrived for Mass fighting raging anger. And then, I listened to the readings and Father's homily…all about love of one's enemies and not seeking revenge. I needed this so badly! I could feel myself letting go of the anger during the liturgy of the word, and by the time we received communion, I was ready to say "amen," knowing what that really means.

This was for Jim and Eileen a moment of deepening conversion, calling upon all they believe and know of Christ's love to guide their response to a demanding situation. They were confronted with the radical expectations of gospel living and were ready to be challenged. Eileen and Jim are not alone in this desire. In fact, many truly wish to live authentic Christian lives and hope their parish will help them to do so.

Jim would tell us that every moment is an opportunity to grow closer to Christ and to be willing to imitate our Master in love and service. When he arrived at church that evening, he was already searching his heart, reminding himself of all that Christ teaches. Listening to the readings and the homily and entering fully into the prayer of the community, Jim drew upon the many ways in which he

---

Transformation: To be transformed is to be completely changed and improved. Embracing the Christian way in all of life's circumstances leads us to be transformed over time, not once and for all, but gradually.

"The gospel speaks across time and space to each human being, each mind, each heart. It asks us what we think about our lives, how we hope, whom we love, and what we live for. If faith is not transforming each heart and life, it is dead."

(**Go and Make Disciples**, p. 9)

continues to grow in Christ. He and Eileen regularly participate in adult faith formation at their parish. Jim is a lector and Eileen is an extraordinary minister of Holy Communion. They serve in a local food pantry, are leaders in a wide range of ministries, and are deeply committed to integrating faith and life. The people around them have witnessed their gradual transformation, and they have become people their family and co-worker seek out for guidance in times of crisis. Jim and Eileen model the kind of lifelong conversion in Christ that parishes hope will be part of each person's life. Fostering such transformation in Christ requires each of us to be on the path of conversion ourselves and to provide opportunities of every sort for those ready to embrace the depth of Christian discipleship, with mind, heart, and hands.

Think of your own experience. When have you experienced a moment of initial or deepening conversion to Christ? Who or what helped you to grow from that experience?

"Jesus set the world on fire, and that blaze goes on even today" (*Go and Make Disciples*, introduction). In the final evaluation, everything that is part of parish life, every act of worship, service, and community, every moment of catechesis, pastoral conversation, or renewal, the real, true goal of it all is to fall in love with God in Christ, and to share that love with others; to be on fire with the Spirit of the Lord.

Lifelong Transformation

The experience of Christ is not a once-in-a-lifetime event, of course, at least not for those who enter the path of discipleship with an open heart and a willing spirit. And so life in the parish is not only aimed at initial experiences of Christ, but toward a lifetime of conversion. The U.S. bishops

---

Conversion: The lifelong process of transformation. Sometimes people speak of being conformed to Christ as a way of saying that following Christ will challenge us to let go of the things in our life that are not leading us to goodness or right relationships. Conversion is an expression of living, explicit, and fruitful faith.

Living faith: is both a gift of God and an authentically human response—a recognition of God's call in one's life and a free decision to follow this call by accepting and living the truth of the gospel; is a searching faith, it "seeks understanding"; is keenly conscious and aware of the power and hold of sin in human life; longs for the fulfillment of eternal life.

Explicit Faith: is rooted in a personal relationship with Jesus lived in the Christian community; is connected to the life, teaching, and mission of the Church; is founded on the word of God and confirmed by the whole Church's supernatural sense of the faith.

Fruitful Faith: enjoys the fruits of the Spirit which are "love, joy, peace, patience, kindness, generosity, faithfulness, gentleness, self-control" (Gal 5:22-23); bears the fruit of justice and compassion; bears the fruit of evangelization.

(Our Hearts Were Burning Within Us, p. 16-20)

---

put it this way in their pastoral letter on evangelization, *Go and Make Disciples*:

> This is crucial: we must be converted—and we must continue to be converted! We must let the Holy Spirit change our lives! We must respond to Jesus Christ. And we must be open to the transforming power of the Holy Spirit who will continue to convert us as we follow Christ. If our faith is alive, it will be aroused again and again as we mature as disciples. (p. 9)

EMBRACE CONVERSION YOURSELF

If you are reading this book, it is probable that you are a parish leader in some fashion. You may be a pastor who is searching for ways to strengthen your parish; you may be a pastoral staff member who needs a few new ideas; maybe you're a parishioner who is part of a committee that will bring recommendations for a pastoral planning project. Whatever your reason for reading, you probably didn't expect to find within this book encouragement for you, encouragement to make a commitment to continue to grow in your love of God. Love of God led you to the ministry that is now your life. God called and continues to call you. The Spirit of our God is your guide, your strength, your light. Your commitment to Christ will make a difference in the lives of those with whom and to whom you minister. So, whatever it takes, commit yourself to falling more deeply in love with God and to being a sign and witness to that love. We cannot give what we do not have; we cannot foster what we do not take seriously ourselves; we cannot urge others to be committed to lifelong conversion if we ourselves are not on that path. As our bishops remind all of us, we must let the Holy Spirit change us and continue to convert us as we follow Christ. When we ourselves are on the path of lifelong transformation, then and only then, may we begin to establish patterns of ongoing conversion for others.

What is it, after all, that you hope will happen as you create a climate in which people may encounter Christ? You know that there are many adults in our parishes who are faithful in coming to Mass, may even be involved in a ministry or organization. They go through the motions and likely wish there was something deeper in their lives. What they seek is a real relationship with Christ, something that hits them where they live, that makes a difference when life is challenging, or adds substance to life when all seems to be well. People want to know God, but many—most if we are really honest—just don't know where to begin.

THE PARADOX OF A LIFE IN CHRIST

There is a paradox in this life in Christ, of course, and people who seek a deep relationship with God intuitively sense the conflicting possibilities. Being drawn into Christ will necessarily draw us out toward others, away from self-concern, and into "other-concern." All the while we sense that embracing God will have astonishing affects in our lives, and we also sense that the change will demand much of us. Sometimes, in an effort to explain what life in Christ holds in store, parish folks fall into "churchy" language that puts off those who are looking for a "real" relationship with "real" implications. Bulletin notices or homilists speak of the paschal mystery (an amazing concept, of course, that takes each of us a lifetime to grasp), rather than saying that Christ's life, ministry, passion, death, and resurrection hold the key for us in the way we live and transcend life now and into eternity. We who lead parishes seem to spend much time telling people what they "should" do, rather than giving them concrete examples of what Christian discipleship "looks like" in real situations. Yet, when we listen, people will tell us that what they most desire is to know that truth and love are real and that God cares more deeply about them than their limited human reasoning can fathom.

The relationship begins for many of us in the waters of baptism in infancy. Others grow in their knowledge and love of God and are initiated into Christ as teens or adults. Some will be strengthened or renewed as Christian disciples through a retreat or renewal process, through sharing the journey of faith with others, and through hearing how Christ has transformed the people around them. For many, the importance of a spiritual director or a small church community cannot be overstated. Just as each of us has been uniquely created in God's image, so each of us must find a different combination of elements to guide us along our path. The parish community that takes the spiritual growth of its members seriously will recognize the need for a variety of processes available to people—at varying times of the year and for varying life stages.

CHANGES HAPPEN GRADUALLY

Benefiting from the witness of others and being invited to witness ourselves, parish leaders begin to see more clearly the shifts that take place in people's lives as they embrace life in Christ. The shifts happen gradually and are ones that have been part of the Christian life from the beginning. In fact, it is easy to see evidence of the growth of the disciples throughout our gospels and the letters of the New Testament.

Witnessing: To witness is to see or experience something and to share your experience with another. A Christian witness shares his or her experience of faith with another, privately or publicly. Parishes seeking to establish stewardship as a way of life often include lay witnesses as part of their annual stewardship formation process.

"Since stewardship is a way of life, and not simply a program of church support, the most important ingredient in any effort to encourage giving of time, talent, and treasure is the personal witness of individuals (clergy, religious, and lay) who have experienced a change of heart as a result of their commitment to stewardship. For this reason, parishes and dioceses are strongly encouraged to ground their stewardship and development programs in the personal witness of the bishop, pastor, parish or diocesan staff, and volunteers."

(Stewardship: A Disciple's Response, p. 59)

Even as we consider the ways in which we will be transformed over time, we remember that we are not alone in the transformation. With the grace and fullness of the Holy Spirit, we are gifted beyond measure. Spirit-filled Christians are given gifts with which to contribute toward the building of God's reign. When we offer our gifts back to the God who gives them to us, there is no limit to what God may do through us! Our parishes will become communities of God-centered people, offering their gifts for the benefit of others. Ever-changing lives of conversion in Christ's love will be filled with generous gratitude.

DEVELOPING A VISION

He brought Simon to Jesus, who looked at him and said,
"You are Simon son of John. You are to be called Cephas,"
which is translated Peter. ~JOHN 1:42

Peter, of course, is an excellent gospel example of this ongoing transformation. Our first encounter with him, as quoted in the beginning of this principle, is his name change. Name changes infer transformation. But Peter's transformation didn't end there. He slips and falls, rises and walks on water, then denies Christ only to be the Rock at the end of it all. How wonderful to have an example of a transformation that isn't a one-time thing. How human! At the end of John's gospel we see the evidence of Peter's transformation. Jesus requires Peter to declare his love, not once but three times. The third time, Peter responds, "Lord, you know everything; you know that I love you." Jesus said to him, "Feed my sheep." After this he said to him, "Follow me" (John 21:17, 19). In what ways does your parish feed the sheep who are yearning to be transformed in Christ?

WHAT THE DOCUMENTS SAY

The *General Directory for Catechesis* makes it clear that "Faith is a gift destined to grow in the hearts of believers. Adhering to Jesus Christ, in fact, sets in motion a process of continuing conversion, which lasts for the whole of life. Those who come to faith are like newborn children, who, little by little, will grow and change into adults, tending toward maturity in Christ." The text goes on to identify key moments in the process such as, "interest in the gospel, conversion, profession of faith, and journeying toward perfection" (#56). Nowhere is it stated that one single event provides for all transformation and conversion. Throughout the document, it is referred to as a lifelong process.

In the *Catechism of the Catholic Church*, we are directed toward an understanding of the lifelong transformation process. "To live, grow, and persevere in the faith until the end we must nourish it with the word of God; we must beg the Lord to increase our faith; it must be 'working through charity,' abounding in hope, and rooted in the faith of the Church" (#162).

Throughout the bishops' documents we get an understanding that this transformation takes place in all ages and stages. In the *National Directory for Catechesis*, each stage is addressed and given goals and tasks.

> Growth in faith is related to human development and passes through stages. Individuals develop as human beings and faithful followers of Christ in different ways and according to their own pace. No matter what style or rate of growth in faith, such growth always means gradually becoming more like Christ. It means growing into communion with the Father and the Son in the Holy Spirit through active participation in the sacraments, the prayer life of the Church, and generous service to others. (p. 187)

Of course, these documents refer to the catechetical nature of our work, which is just part of the bigger picture. In *Evangelii Nuntiandi*, Pope Paul VI gives us this reminder of the ongoing nature of our work:

> Nevertheless the Church does not feel dispensed from paying unflagging attention also to those who have received the faith and who have been in contact

with the gospel often for generations. Thus she seeks to deepen, consolidate, nourish, and make ever more mature the faith of those who are already called the faithful or believers, in order that they may be so still more. (54)

He calls us to remember that our work within is equally important to our work outside of the Church.

What vision of a transformative parish emerges for you from these documents? If you were asked to describe this vision in one sentence, what would you say?

EXPLORING SUCCESSFUL PRACTICE

Practice One: Let the Catechumenate Be Your Model

"The model for all catechesis is the baptismal catechumenate when by specific formation an adult converted to belief is brought to explicit profession of baptismal faith during the Paschal Vigil. This catechumenal formation should inspire the other forms of catechesis in both their objectives and in their dynamism" (*General Directory for Catechesis*, #59). Catechesis that is inspired by the catechumenate will be shaped by its elements. Those who seek to structure parish life so it leads to lifelong transformation and to stewardship as a way of life will do well to look to the catechumenate for ways to foster ongoing conversion in Christ.

One of the most effective ways to foster faith that is integrated into real life is to provide catechesis that is deeply imbued with the rhythm of the liturgical seasons,

Catechumenate: Often referred to as the "RCIA," the catechumenate is the process by which people prepare for initiation into Christ's life and into the Catholic Christian community. The Rite of Christian Initiation of Adults (RCIA) is the collection of rites we celebrate with those who prepare for baptism, confirmation, and Eucharist (catechumens), those who are baptized in other Christian denominations and now wish to be received into the full communion of the Catholic Church, or those who were baptized as Catholics but never completed their initiation (candidates). The catechumenate process is marked by distinct stages along the way and is multi-faceted, including a strong connection to the Sunday celebration and liturgical seasons, rootedness in prayer, discernment about the connections between faith and life, and an outpouring of Christian service, integration of a spirituality toward justice and peace, and the adoption of a Christian worldview.

equipping people to feel that rhythm "in their bones." Schedule catechesis gatherings (times when people of all ages come together for faith formation) just before the new season begins; break open the meaning, symbols, and ritual actions of the season, and provide seasonal materials for your households: reflective materials, discussion questions, or ideas for a seasonal prayer center for the home. For example, a brief reflection for each week of Advent could be placed in your Sunday bulletin or as an insert or handout. The reflection material would have a strong connection to how people might change their behavior as a result of their faith in Christ, and would offer ideas for things people could do in their households to reinforce what they are experiencing at the Sunday celebration of the Eucharist. *Form people through and for prayer.* The life of the disciple must be rooted in an active and varied life of prayer. We sometimes forget that prayer forms us. The more we offer people a variety of experiences of prayer, and help them understand the prayer they take part in, the more likely they will be to carry those experiences into their daily lives. Expose children to the liturgy of the hours, through adapted morning prayer, for example, and they will share their rich prayer life with their parents. Provide materials for household use, and members will be drawn to additional reading, study, and practice.

Begin or continue to use the Question of the Week as a way to provide ongoing faith reflection for parishioners that is connected to the Sunday gospel. At the end of the homily, or at the end of the Mass just prior to dismissal, offer a question for the community's reflection in the coming week. The question can be printed in the bulletin (sometimes on the cover of the bulletin) and used at parish meetings, small faith community gatherings, at the beginning of faith formation assemblies, and in households at the dinner table or for individual reflection. The question is not a content-checking question, but rather invites people to look at their own experience of life in relationship to the gospel. Some parishes offer time for people to linger just after Mass to discuss the question together. (For more information on the Question of the Week, including Web sites and resources to support this practice, go to our Web site www. thegenerousheart.com.)

Place the Church's sacramental life at the center of your catechesis. Parishes that offer "why we do what we do" events of one sort or another report an always-strong response from people who want to better understand the meaning of our liturgical celebrations. Offer walk-throughs (not dialogue or instructional liturgies) of the Mass, or the sacraments of initiation or the sacraments of healing. Invite people to gather around the font to learn more about what baptism calls us to be, why we celebrate baptism during Sunday Mass, and why we bless ourselves with the baptismal water as we enter church or during the sprinkling rite. Invite people to bring their questions about your celebrations with them and invite them to share how such catechesis changes the way they pray as a result.

Open some sessions of the catechumenate to the adults of the parish. Choose a few topics each year that are sure to be covered in the catechumenate, and then open those sessions to the community. How often do we hear folks who have been Catholic all of their lives speak of a desire to experience the catechumenate? They hear of the conversion that takes place around tables, in deep conversation and study, and they wish for such an experience themselves. So invite them in occasionally! The result will be a stronger connection between the catechumens, candidates, and the rest of the community, and the faith of all will be strengthened.

Draw people more deeply into the community of believers. Sometimes we forget that the simple act of sharing a meal can be formative, especially when we build in the potential for conversation and the sharing of living faith. For example, hold a potluck supper and share meal stories. Call the gathering "Eating our Way through the Gospels" or something like that, and invite people to share their faith around a gospel narrative at which Jesus sat at table with friends, sinners, or outsiders. Remember that when we play together, we experience the joyful and compassionate presence of Christ among us!

Practice Two: Take Time for Renewal

We cannot underestimate the power and importance of offering opportunities for people to encounter and be encountered by Christ through retreats and/or a renewal process. The sad reality is that many who are with us regularly have never had an intense experience of Christ's presence in their lives, or they have let this relationship grow stagnant and thus the fire of faith has become cold. When the individual begins to sense God calling him or her deeper, a retreat or renewal experience will be transformative, and as individuals are transformed, so will be the parish community.

Practice Three: Form the Leaders

Study and reflect on the Church's documents: Find a parishioner who is gifted at identifying key concepts or sections of a document, and invite that member to create a formation/reflection piece for leadership groups. Just a paragraph or two at a time will be sufficient to form the leaders in the vision of the Church in relationship to an aspect of our lives as a parish community. With that understanding, leaders can be asked to reflect on the vision that is presented, offering their insights into current parish practice and to possible strategies or goals for the future of the parish.

Network with other parishes' leaders and with diocesan or regional leadership: Parishioner leaders often benefit from conversing with counterparts in neighboring parishes or by attending diocesan or regional formation days. Not only will they find common struggles and learn of possible strategies for growth, but the investment of time and attention to their formation by the parish/pastor/pastoral staff says much about the leader's value as a person and as a person of ministry.

Invite leaders to an annual formation day in which a visitor is invited to offer a message of encouragement, challenge, and formation. If funds are limited for such a day, arrange to trade time with a leader in a neighboring parish, or invite someone from your own parish to prepare a reflection or catechetical segment using a published resource.

Practice Four: Create Small Groups

The importance of small groups in the lives of many Christians cannot be understated. Small church groups, renewal groups, and reading circles offer people a consistent network of support, formation, and challenge. There is a significant relationship between small group membership and engagement: members of small groups are more than twice as likely to be engaged in their faith community as those who are not in a small group. While it is difficult to know whether their involvement is a result of their already-developing engagement or their engagement is a result of their small-group experience, creating, fostering, and supporting small groups is vitally important (Winseman, p. 136–140). Small-group members often comment that it is their group that reminds them that discipleship is a lifelong journey requiring commitment.

Practice Five: Witness Talks

Providing opportunities for people to witness to their faith and the ways their faith is affecting their lives can make a big difference to both individuals and the parish community. Many parishes find it beneficial to invite parishioners to share their stories of God's love in their lives with one another through retreat experiences, in small faith communities, in sharing sessions on the weekends, and sometimes by addressing the assembly before or at the end of Mass. Think of ways to incorporate faith sharing into your intergenerational gatherings and sacramental preparation, too. Also try to regularly share stories of ways parishioners are living their faith in your bulletin or parish newsletter.

Hearing others' stories of faith helps us to remember that life in Christ is an everyday reality. We can be inspired by acts of courage and awed by compassion, encouraged by simple moments of faith, and struck by the ways in which God walks with us during times of trial. Through stories of faith we can be urged to act justly and to live in solidarity with the small and weak, and we can see love in the face of a neighbor.

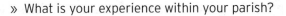

» What is your experience within your parish?

» What practices are you aware of that contribute to people being transformed in Christ throughout their lives?

» What ideas do you have for ways to build upon what is already taking place within your parish, or for developing new practices to enhance lifelong transformation within your community?

PRINCIPLE 3

Faith Meets Life

He said to her, "Daughter, your faith has made you well."
~MARK 5:34

Faith meets *life* as the parish helps to equip people to live as disciples in the whole of their lives, in their homes, workplaces, neighborhoods, and world. This is principle three.

Ramon was discussing ways he might become involved in parish ministry with a Gifts Coordinator. He said,

My wife and I have always tried to continue learning about our faith. It's so much easier here than it was in our last parish! The first month that we were here, there was some sort of gathering every week, sometimes more often. It's good to know that there are others who are committed to growing stronger in their faith. You can really feel the strength of the Spirit when we pray together or talk about what is happening in our lives at table discussions. Last night at the dinner table at home, Nicole and I started talking about what a blessing this is in our lives. It is making a difference, being able to share faith with others and then seeing the connections with what we have talked about and what is happening at work or at home.

Ramon continued,

> We've met people of all ages, too. The younger couples inspire me with the ways they help their children grow in faith, and the older couples encourage us, telling us to savor every moment, and weather life's storms with prayer. I met a single man last week who spoke of the parish as his family. He said that he invites coworkers to come to socials here, and they are amazed at how welcome they feel. He said one of them told him, "if I knew church could be like this, I'd come to church more often!" He told me how much richer his life is now that there are ways for him to study scripture and talk with others about their lives in light of their faith. The wonderful thing was, the next Sunday, we sat together at Mass; how good it is to grow in faith together!

WHAT PEOPLE DESIRE

Listen to people talk about what they desire from their parish. Most, like Ramon, will tell us, if we're willing to listen, that they hope for help in making connections between their faith and their life. Even better, if the parish is going to meet people's needs, it will equip them to meet the challenges of daily life, to make Christian decisions in the face of a world that suggests there is an easy answer for everything. They want to fully integrate the whole of their lives, as people of faith, as disciples of Christ. Those who are parents want help in raising their children with Christ at the center of their family. Those who are single desire a community in which they may be refreshed and rooted. Older members want to know that there will be people to

> Think of your own experience: How does your faith affect the way you live your life? Who or what helps you to make the important connections between faith in Christ and daily living?

walk with them no matter what life holds for them and their families. In brief, people want their parish community to be the place in which faith becomes real, a place in which there are others like themselves—people who want to grow in faith, in understanding, in relationship with God and others.

Anyone who has been involved in parish ministry for any length of time knows that helping people form such connections is not simple. In fact, the challenges are great. Structuring parish practices that encourage and challenge people to live generous, God-centered lives requires reflection, forethought, and planning. Such parish practice will not develop overnight, and once we begin, we must be ever-vigilant or the progress we make will quickly slip away. This is not parish leadership for the faint of heart!

WHAT THE DATA TELL US

Studies of Catholics of all generations and of those who leave active practice of Catholicism provide important insights as we determine pastoral approaches and priorities. For example, a 2005 study sponsored by the *National Catholic Reporter* indicates that even among those who were identified as possessing a high commitment to the Church, 41% said that Catholic Church leaders are out of touch with reality. That number more than doubles to 85% among Catholics with a low level of commitment to the Church (September 30, 2005). While many areas of life might be included in such a statement, the statistics seem to echo the sentiments of many in our pews each week who ask us to help them make real connections between their faith and their lives.

Parishes seeking to serve young adults can provide "support for family life," says Dr. Dean Hoge, a sociologist at the Catholic University of America. "Anything that involves children, such as religious education programs, schools, teen ministry, or family camps will have an appeal to young families. Parish leaders need to be bold, experiment, and find out what works to attract this key group," he says (Peter Feuerherd, "Where are those missing Catholics?" *Church*, Spring 2007, p. 8).

Family Religious Involvement and the Quality of Family Relationships for Early Adolescents points to the importance of youth ministry and of the involvement of Catholic parents, reporting that "Catholic teens with involved Catholic parents are more observant and interested in religious faith, noting that one way to have an impact on future generations is to educate parents in the faith" ("Benefits for Teens in Religiously Involved Families," *The CARA Report*, Vol. 9, No. 1, Summer 2003).

Those seeking a new faith community want to know that there are others like themselves who are committed to spiritual growth and that the parish is a place in which they can learn and grow (Winseman, p. 105–111).

Catechesis or Faith Formation "aims to bring about in
the believer an ever more mature faith in Jesus Christ, a
deeper knowledge and love of his person and message,
and a firm commitment to follow him. With God's grace,
catechesis develops initial faith, nourishes the Christian
life, and continually unfolds the mystery of Christ until the
believer willingly becomes his disciple."

(**National Directory for Catechesis**, 19A)

Catechesis or Faith Formation:
>> promotes knowledge of the faith;
>> promotes a knowledge of the meaning of the liturgy
and the sacraments;
>> promotes moral formation in Jesus Christ;
>> teaches the Christian how to pray with Christ;
>> prepares the Christian to live in community and to
participate actively in the life and mission of the
Church;
>> promotes a missionary spirit that prepares the faithful
to be present as Christians in society.

FAITH FORMATION STRENGTHENS DAILY LIFE

All of the above suggests the importance of parish practices
and the availability of lifelong catechesis that strengthens
people to live their faith in their homes, workplaces, and
neighborhoods. Parishes that establish a regular rhythm of
family and adult faith formation find that such gatherings
have multiple benefits: people deepen their love of the
Lord, their understanding of the faith, their relationships
with each other; their comfort in inviting others to join
them. Over time people develop a sure footing in faith that

anchors them through the joys and sorrows, the ordinary and extraordinary moments of life. While parishes may develop myriad opportunities for adult and/or intergenerational catechesis over time, beginning to address the desires of people to grow closer to Christ and each other need not be overwhelming. In fact, the simpler the beginning, the more likely it will be to sustain and develop opportunities to meet the needs of the community.

Ramon's delight in finding his parish to be a place in which there are many opportunities to grow in faith with others inspires us with hope that his parish's practices are not the exception but rather the norm!

DEVELOPING A VISION

He said to her, "Daughter, your faith has made you well."
~MARK 5:34

So, as in the case of the hemorrhaging woman, our faith saves us from whatever is ailing us and allows us to live our daily life. Remember the story? The woman had been hemorrhaging for years and had heard about Jesus. She wasn't able to face him but "came up behind him in the crowd and touched his cloak." What faith! She thought that just by touching his cloak she'd be better. She also knew that she, an unclean woman, was making Jesus unclean in her touching. Still, when he asked who had touched him, she steps forward. Instead of being punished, her faith is announced and Jesus ends his address to her with "go in peace, and be healed of your disease" (Mark 5:34). In order for her to live her life, she needed the contact with Jesus. Through her encounter with him, she was able to go into her life and live it in peace, which is what our parishioners desire. They are looking for encounters that will empower them (and us) to do the right thing, say the right words, and be the right people. Even, or especially, in the challenges of life—pain, defeat, etc.—we find meaning and purpose through our faith in Jesus. How does your parish help people encounter Christ in all of the stages of their lives, in "real" ways?

WHAT THE DOCUMENTS SAY

We are challenged to create an environment in which people encounter Jesus Christ, are empowered to live our daily lives with him, and are called to respond to the love we know in Christ by moving beyond ourselves toward others. Our Church's documents call us to be open to the challenges that arise from living our faith.

In the documents of Vatican II these challenges are addressed in *Gaudium et spes* (Church in the Modern World). As Bill Huebsch notes in *Vatican II in Plain English: The Constitutions* (Thomas More, 1997, p. 121–22), "*Gaudium et spes* is truly an international, transglobal, ecumenical document summarizing what we humans believe about ourselves...(it) hopes that we will now proceed with richer relationships among ourselves, more economic justice, less threat of war, a more humane use of technology, and a generally more noble lifestyle for all people." The document itself goes into great detail about the challenges of being a person of faith in the modern world. One of the proponents of *Gaudium et spes* was the Cardinal of Milan, Giovanni Battista Montini who would, a few months after speaking in favor of the document, be elected to the papacy and take the name Paul VI. Ten years later, realizing that there was an ongoing need to address modern life, Pope Paul VI delivered the apostolic exhortation *Evangelii Nuntiandi* in which he stated:

> This is precisely what we wish to do here, at the end of this Holy Year during which the Church, "striving to proclaim the Gospel to all people,"[3] has had the single aim of fulfilling her duty of being the messenger of the Good News of Jesus Christ—the Good News proclaimed through two fundamental commands: "Put on the new self"[4] and "Be reconciled to God."[5]
>
> We wish to do so on this tenth anniversary of the closing of the Second Vatican Council, the objectives of which are definitively summed up in this single one: *to make the Church of the twentieth century ever better fitted for proclaiming the Gospel to the people of the twentieth century.* (italics added)

We as Church have continued to follow this call not just to proclaim the gospel but to help people live as gospel. In *Renewing the Vision* the goals of youth ministry echo this primary goal: "To empower young people to live as disciples of Jesus Christ in our world today" (p. 9). Furthermore, in *Sons and Daughters of the Light*, the third goal with young adults is "To invite young adults, through healthy relationships, work, and studies, to embrace the mission of Christ to promote the building of the kingdom of God in the world today, thereby bringing about the transformation of society" (p. 36).

Our connection to society is made clear in the *Catechism of the Catholic Church*: "the human person needs to live in society. Society is not for him an extraneous addition but a requirement of his nature. Through the exchange with others, mutual service and dialogue with his brethren, man develops his potential; he thus responds to his vocation" (#1879). Furthermore it states that we have responsibility and are called to participation in society (in articles 1913–17). A few points from these articles bear special mention:

✠ "It is necessary that all participate" (#1913)

✠ "As far as possible citizens should take an active part in public life" (#1915)

✠ "As with any ethical obligation, the participation of all in realizing the common good calls for a continually renewed conversion of the social partners" (#1916)

The *National Directory for Catechesis* seems to echo both other documents and the desire of every faithful follower: "The society to which they (men and women) belong should inspire them to develop themselves as followers of Christ and to develop their families, their communities, and their cultures" (p. 169).

Having said all this, we need to examine the role we have in providing the connections from what takes place "in church" to what people do "in real life."

EXPLORING SUCCESSFUL PRACTICE

Practice One: Bring Liturgy to Life!

Live the liturgy! Offer ways for people to learn about our sacramental prayer, to reflect on their experience of the liturgy, and to see the ways in which the Sunday celebration of the Eucharist is both nourishment and challenge for daily living.

Bring liturgy home to the parish. Invite people to support each other in varying life circumstances in light of their experience of liturgy. Life stage groups are ideal for such discussion: parenting groups, men's or women's groups, senior gatherings, married couples, singles, divorced and separated individuals. There is power in shared experience.

Practice Two: Create Time to Gather

Occasional gatherings at the parish can help to equip adults to live their faith in myriad ways at home, in the workplace, or neighborhood. Providing ways for adults to be together socially or for faith formation that includes

What vision of a parish of living faith emerges for you in these documents? If you were asked to describe this vision in one sentence, what would you say?

discussion or sharing is of great benefit to many adults. Hearing that others share similar challenges in applying faith to real-life decisions can make all the difference for people who are ready to deepen their relationship with Christ.

Bulletin or web-based catechesis: The impact of a simple question or brief reflective or instructional paragraph is difficult to measure, but certain to be worth the little time it takes to develop. People often look for something that can provide just a little instruction or reflection that can be used at home, in the time and space available in the midst of daily life.

Practice Three: Offer Liturgical Catechesis

It has been said that if a parish hopes to design a church building that will meet its needs and inspire its people, those who are involved in the design process should go to the Sacred *Triduum* (Holy Thursday, Good Friday, the Easter Vigil) to have a full appreciation of what is required. The same could be said if we hope to structure parish life in ways that will possess the depth, breadth, and height of what is needed in order to form people in living discipleship. The celebration of the Mass of the Lord's Supper brings us face to face with the gift, blessing, and challenge of the Eucharist, through word, bread, wine, and washing of feet. Through the Passion of our Lord, we encounter the fullness of God's love for us in Christ, we place ourselves at the foot of the cross, penitent and struck by our frailty, and we offer prayers for the needs of all in our world. In the great Vigil, we are immersed in the story of salvation, initiated into Christ's death and life, confirmed in the Spirit, and fed at the feast of the Lord. Easter morning's glory is our own and is our reminder that the Christian life always holds the promise of the resurrection.

Parish life patterned after the Triduum will hold nothing back in the ways of service, solidarity, passion and compassion, beginnings and renewal. We will find ways to form and be formed for discipleship within the parish and beyond it.

If the Eucharist is to be the central moment of our lives in Christ, we must find ways in which to "bring it home"; ways that virtually every person in the pew can employ to better understand and be confronted with love, blessed, broken, and poured out. Devote a series of catechetical gatherings to explore the Mass and sacraments, feasts and seasons of our life together. Keep them simple. A few key concepts, explored through a variety of ways will be much appreciated. First, help people understand why we do what we do. Then later explore the depth of our sacramental action in a variety of ways. Don't worry about repetition; hearing the same concepts at different points in our lives is a bit like hearing the Sunday readings over a three-year span. Don't presume knowledge. However, it is appreciated when examples are offered that connect the concepts to daily life. Parents who come to an intergenerational event will appreciate something to take home with them, to explore the same topics with their children in the coming weeks.

People deeply appreciate the opportunity to gather for or to be formed for fuller participation in a variety of styles of prayer, especially celebrations that are native to ethnic groups represented in the parish. Not only is this beneficial to the people whose traditions are being carried into new generations, but introducing prayer forms to the whole community is a sign of the ways in which we all belong to God and to one another.

People also benefit from conversations about what "sacrament" means, and how our lives are meant to be "sacramental" in a mirroring of the sacraments that are part of our Catholic Christian life. People are moved by reflections on the meaning of "remembrance" and every time this topic arises, people will remark how helpful it is for them to better understand that when we pray the prayers of consecration we are not simply telling the story of something that happened many centuries ago, but rather are remembering the saving acts of Christ here and now. Those actions are made present to us in sacrament and sign in this present age.

People enjoy intergenerational catechesis assemblies that are active, in which learning centers are used or demonstrations offered that include the opportunity for questions and interaction. A regular rhythm of assemblies of this nature, combined with a variety of ways for people to prepare for the Sunday celebration is making a difference in the lives of many parishioners. People are finding that just a few such moments can really help the Eucharist to come alive and be central in their daily living.

Practice Four: Use the Tools of the Day

A *weekly e-mail communication* helps to keep parishioners connected to each other in the midst of their daily lives. This mid-week communication can be very simple. Include a few sentences of prayer or reflection, a list of the activities that are taking place at the parish for the remainder of the week, a list of those who are ill or who have died, with requests for prayers. Links or brief promotions can be included to highlight special events or upcoming opportunities for involvement or formation.

> » What is your experience within your parish?

> » What practices are you aware of that equip people to live their faith?

> » What ideas do you have for ways to build upon what is already taking place within your parish, or for developing new practices to help people to live their daily lives as disciples of the Lord?

PRINCIPLE 4

Full, Conscious, and Active Participation

Blessed is the one who will dine in the kingdom of God.
~LUKE 14:15

Form people to fully, consciously, and actively *participate* in all of parish life, as a sign and witness of Christ's presence. This is the fourth principle.

Father Jan Kevin Schmidt was invited to speak at the fall archdiocesan convocation of priests. He was specifically asked to describe what happened in his parish, transforming it from one that was divided and in debt to one that had just completed a major renovation of facilities, thanks to the faithful stewardship of parishioners. Father Jan described what took place in this way:

> When I arrived at the parish, I found much that was discouraging and didn't know where to turn for help. I read anything I could find that might provide a clue, talked with other pastors and with parish leaders, and I prayed a lot. Then one day, I found myself reflecting on the liturgical principle of "full, conscious, and active participation," and I realized that this principle goes beyond ritual enactment. It is a principle for

the Christian life and for the life of the parish. When people are invited and expected to fully, consciously, and actively participate in the life of their parish community, wonderful things begin to happen, and that is what took place in my parish. Now, twelve years later, we have literally thousands of parishioners actively involved in ministry. Parish leaders are in place to advise and guide every aspect of our lives as a community of believers, and people pour themselves out in service. Our celebrations of the Eucharist are central to all of this—people are living what they celebrate, and are growing deeply as God's own.

Father Jan's insights have guided his parish to embrace discipleship wholeheartedly, with the principle of full, conscious, and active participation as a key to the ways in which members view their lives together. Fashioning parish life and practice on this principle, of course, will have striking implications for the ways in which we structure leadership and organization within our parishes.

Fully Participating

What is key to developing a fully participative parish? We begin by developing the firm belief that everyone in the community belongs and has something to offer. Unfortunately, typical parish practice often contradicts such a belief. We speak of the importance of parishioner involvement, yet how often do we *value* parishioner input or suggestions when they challenge us or ask us to stretch and grow? The research on engagement indicates that parishioners need to know what is expected of them and to believe that their opinions count in order to form those important emotional connections in the community. Both are instrumental in establishing an environment in which people know that they are *valued* by the community (Winseman, p. 87). It isn't that people expect all of parish life to be exactly as they would like; they recognize that communal life requires each person to die to self a bit for the sake of the community. They understand themselves as being of value, however, when their contributions are acknowledged. They come to see that belonging to the community has a *value* in their lives when they know what is expected of them, and what they can expect in return. Expressing such expectations must be done with care, of course. If we approach people with musts, shoulds, and have-to's, our words are likely to fall on deaf ears. Articulating what is expected of parishioners and inviting their partnership in a way that helps them to see that their full participation is important to the community (and to their own lives) is essential.

Think of your own experience: When have you experienced full, conscious, and active participation in your parish? Who or what drew you into this experience?

A parish leadership structure and practice that reflects the belief that all are of value and that their contributions are appreciated is most effective. For example, does the parish have a pastoral plan that has been developed by listening to parishioners' desires and hopes for their community? How are new ministries begun and how are they sustained?

When a new ministry begins, are parishioners given the opportunity to acknowledge those who are dedicating a portion of their time and their gifts in service? Are all aspects of parish life guided through consultation with parish leaders, and are adjustments made when consensus toward change is reached (provided, of course that the change is not in conflict with Canon Law or sound theological principles)?

Gratitude and the Generous Heart

The importance of forming people in a spirituality of gratitude and responsive generosity becomes key to the life of individuals and of the community as full, conscious, and active participation in the parish becomes the goal. When people see that the parish is responsive to the needs of people within the community and especially of those who are poor in their neighborhoods, country, and world, they will see their blessings more clearly and are more likely to respond generously. Members who make recommendations and are involved in decision making, and those who see that others are involved as parishioner leaders, grow not only in their investment in the parish, but as children of God who experience the grace of God's presence in their lives, poured out in loving service.

Evangelization and Discipleship

Examine every practice and aspect of your parish's life through the lens of evangelization and discipleship. We will develop additional thoughts about discipleship in the next principle, so let us consider evangelization here. Often when we speak of evangelization, we think of attracting

Evangelization: When we evangelize, we share the good news of Jesus Christ with others. "In summary, the new evangelization is primarily the 'clear and unequivocal proclamation of the person of Jesus Christ, that is, the preaching of his name, his teaching, his life, his promises and the kingdom which he has gained for us by his paschal mystery'" (**National Directory for Catechesis**, 17A). The essential elements of evangelization include:

» missionary activity directed toward non-believers or those who live in religious indifference;

» the initial proclamation of the gospel;

» initial catechetical activity for those who choose the gospel or need to complete their initiation;

» pastoral activity directed toward those of mature Christian faith

(**National Directory for Catechesis**, 17C)

the un-churched or those who no longer actively practice the faith. This is one aspect of evangelization, of course. However, the Church's writings on evangelization suggest a much broader context, and it is that context we will explore here.

EVANGELIZING POTENTIAL

Virtually every moment of our lives in parish community holds evangelizing possibilities. As we keep the goal of the fully participative parish in our mind's eye, and we remember that when people are engaged in the parish they are more likely to be drawn into Christ's life, it will be important for us to be mindful of the evangelizing dimension of the faith community. The community itself is evangelizing, particularly when parish life is structured to foster full participation. The Eucharist and the sacramental life of the Church are evangelizing, especially when the liturgy is celebrated well. As we have already discussed, sacramental preparation can be evangelizing when we recall the beneficial balance between content and formation in faith, between teaching and drawing people into a life of conversion. The moments in the lives of individuals that mark change, transition, death, or life are also evangelizing moments. Think of the potential to draw people more deeply into the life of Christ and the community through funerals, welcome ministry, blessings of expectant parents, children and youth who are preparing to receive the sacraments of initiation, and anointing those who are ill or who face surgery.

LIFE STAGES AND TRANSITIONS

We must mention here the power of viewing life stages and transitions as springboards for evangelization. For example, it makes a rather remarkable impact when parents see the parish as a partner with them in forming their children in the faith. Through frank conversation in which adults are invited to ask questions and discuss real-life connections, families will be ready to embrace sacramental living. Parents are much more likely to return for additional adult or intergenerational faith formation opportunities, or to read and explore on their own, if they have experienced the power of such catechesis. The catechesis then becomes evangelizing, and the result is a generation of adults and children who embrace sacramental living.

BECOMING SACRAMENTAL PEOPLE

When our parishes are filled with people who are striving to live Eucharistic lives, to be sacramental people, we begin to see the real implications of Christian initiation. The community, as a living extension of the Body of Christ, will draw others into deep and lasting relationship, beyond what the surrounding culture can offer. The people of St. Gerard Majella in Port Jefferson Station, New York, speak of experiences similar to what Father Jan shares. They tell us that as people have become more emotionally connected and more engaged in the life of the parish, they have begun to notice marked differences in people's lives. People who are offered job transfers say no so they can stay connected to the parish. Adults bring their aging parents to live with them, in part because they know the parish will assist them as needed. Young people identify themselves as members of the parish, rather than speaking of their geographic location. As people grasp that they are initiated into Christ, of which the parish is the living embodiment, they want to continue to be immersed deeply in this life, and to draw others to the same experience.

No longer is initiation an abstract notion that arises from documents or prayer texts; rather, it is a living experience, celebrated at the Eucharist.

DEVELOPING A VISION

Blessed is the one who will dine in the kingdom of God.
~LUKE 14:15

When Jesus told the parable of the Great Feast, it was an indictment of those who were aware of him but failed to respond. In the parable, a man invited many people to a feast and they had a number of excuses for not attending. None of the excuses was acceptable to the man (even though they were reasonable). Therefore he sent his servants out and invited "the poor, the crippled, the blind, and the lame" (Luke 14:21), and then he extended this invitation even beyond his normal boundaries. Some of our parishioners are beyond the highways and hedgerows. Those people with excuses for not attending the feast (in the gospel story) were dealt with harshly. This helps us to see the importance of providing ample opportunities that alleviate the need for excuses. It also points to the need for those who hear the invitation to respond. Jesus makes the point that participation must be full, conscious, and active. Are we going into and beyond the highways and hedgerows to invite members into parish life?

WHAT THE DOCUMENTS SAY

The *Decree On the Apostolate of the Laity* begins with a statement on the importance of the participation of all in the life of the Church:

> To intensify the apostolic activity of the people of God (1), the most holy synod earnestly addresses itself to the laity, whose proper and indispensable role in the mission of the Church has already been dealt with in other documents (2). The apostolate of the laity derives from their Christian vocation and the Church can never be without it. Sacred Scripture clearly shows how spontaneous and fruitful such activity was at the very beginning of the Church. (cf. Acts 11:19–21; 18:26; Rom 16:1–16; Phil 4:3)

This Vatican II document let us know that the Church cannot live without the participation of the laity. *Vatican II in Plain English* provides helpful insight: "One thing became clear during the Second Vatican Council: laypeople, together with the clergy, bear co-responsibility for the work of the Church, its renewal, and its future. Despite nearly two thousand years of 'lay participation' in the ministry of the Church, it was not until this council in the mid-twentieth century that this role was examined, affirmed, and expanded" (p. 17).

Many of the goals set forth by the bishops in documents such as *Renewing the Vision* and *Sons and Daughters of the Light* include this concept as a primary goal for work with youth and young adults. But their pastoral letter, *Stewardship: A Disciple's Response*, really brings the point of full, conscious, and active participation into a blazing light. They write:

> And what do Christians bring to the Eucharistic celebration and join there with Jesus' offering? Their lives as Christian disciples; their personal vocations and the stewardship they have exercised regarding them; their individual contributions to the great work of restoring all things in Christ. Disciples give thanks to God for gifts received and strive to share them with others. That is why, as Vatican II says of the Eucharist, "if this celebration is to be sincere and thorough, it must lead to works of charity and mutual help, as well as to missionary activity and to different forms of Christian witness." (p. 34)

Thus a mutual relationship is established. Individuals need to participate and the Church needs them to do so. "The

What vision of a fully participative parish emerges for you from the quote above? If you were asked to describe this vision in one sentence, what would you say?

parish, then, provides the place, persons, and means to summon and sustain adults in lifelong conversion of heart, mind, and life. It is, 'without doubt, the most important locus in which the Christian community is formed and expressed'" (*Our Hearts Were Burning Within Us*, p. 117). One of the goals of adult catechesis is to "promote and support active membership in the Christian community. As adult believers, we learn and live our faith *as active members of the Church*" (p. 70).

EXPLORING SUCCESSFUL PRACTICE

Practice One: Allow People to Get Involved

People who make the shift to living discipleship through active participation in the life of the parish community want to *offer their insights and to be part of decision-making processes*. The Gallup research tells us that one of the important factors that leads to parishioner engagement is knowing that their opinions count and that their contributions are valued (Winseman, 82–83). Sometimes this is a difficult shift for people who are already involved in parish leadership. Remember those people who resisted widening the circles? It is not always easy to hear and respond to the ideas of newcomers, especially when what is being suggested has been tried in some form already— and failed. Sometimes an idea that was met with a ho-hum response at one point may find energetic acclamations just a few years later. Trying something that seems to have merit but only spotty support may take a bit of resolve on our part; listening to the ideas of those who seem all too critical may be difficult; but the very act of hearing, offering the opportunity to become involved in solutions, and to plan with all of the community in mind, is grace-filled and a sure sign of a parish willing to step out in faith.

Include a weekly financial report in the bulletin, including reports on special expenses the parish has faced or ministry projects supported through financial giving. The financial transparency of weekly reports on Sunday contributions shows the financial state of the parish visually and helps parishioners know that they are trusted members of the parish family. Just as children feel a sense of inclusion when their input is sought before a family vacation, each member of our parish family needs to have the opportunity to offer input and to know that his or her contributions are valued, as is each member.

Practice Two: Implement Your Pastoral Plan

The book of Proverbs reminds us that "without vision, the people will perish." A pastor once told his pastoral council that "without vision, the parish will perish." Having a vision, however, is only effective when we take the next step and allow that vision to become a pastoral plan that includes clear goals and do-able objectives. Sometimes the pastor and pastoral leaders must first clarify the vision that will guide the development of a plan; at other times, a vision has emerged over time, and the parish has a guiding mission/vision statement. Once the vision becomes clear, it is time to draw parishioner leaders together and invite them to initiate a pastoral planning process.

Depending on your parish structure and experience with pastoral planning, you may wish to find a good facilitator for the whole process. The plan should emerge from conversations with parishioner-leaders, be rooted in sound Catholic theology, sacred scripture, Church documents, and it should build upon the experience of others (as in this book). The value of collecting ideas from others is that your leadership groups can prepare in advance, with all participants sharing a common vision to direct your collective work.

Invite parishioners who have experienced a variety of parish ministries, as participants, leaders, and through receiving the ministry to be part of the planning process. If you have commissions or committees, some of the input-gathering and early goal development can be done in those groups. They can share their insights, as well as the information they have gathered with your team, for use during the planning process.

The importance of this listening phase cannot be minimized. Parishioners will feel valued and often have important insights to share. Later development of new ministries or changes in current practices will be much more widely accepted if parishioners have had a part in the planning from the beginning. Inviting their ideas and asking for their prayers throughout the process will insure that the plan will take shape in ways that may be surprising and are sure to guide your parish well. Be sure to communicate the plan to the parish as a whole when it is ready to be implemented. For example, a parish developed a small booklet that reminded parishioners of the planning process, reported the goals that had been developed, with the time frame in which the goals would be initiated, and questions for parishioners to use to reflect on how each person or household was contributing to the goals as they were stated. Parishioners were deeply appreciative of the process and the communication, and the parish benefited from the commitment of individuals and of the community as the plan unfolded.

If you have members who have expertise in project management or similar professional roles, invite their participation and/or leadership. Parishioners are often thrilled to be invited to offer their professional experience for the benefit of their parish community.

As you continue reading and reflecting on the material in this book, consider the ways in which you will share what you are learning with others, and how the vision you develop together will guide your parish toward a pastoral plan, or toward implementing a plan that is already in place. Are there additional people who should be invited to join your team now? Would it be of benefit to ask other parishioner leaders to study the principles and to offer their insights as you proceed? Who could be invited to acquire this vision with you? Invite those people to reflect on the vision in relation to the current status of life in the parish: What is already in place within the parish that contributes to the vision? What is lacking? Are there elements that are no longer needed or viable? How could you begin to make the shift from where you are as a parish to the vision you are coming to hold in common?

The flow will often look like this:

Vision → Current status in relationship to the Vision → Goals related to the Vision → Actionable Objectives related to the Goals → Strategies for achieving the Objectives → Celebration of the completion of the Plan and the life in Christ that will come!

Practice Three: Communication

Last year, a parish formed a marketing team. It isn't that they need to "market" the parish exactly, but the team realized that there are parishioners who are gifted in the areas of communication, advertising, design, and web-based communication. They invited a small group to come together to discuss ways in which communication could be improved within the parish, and the discussion was so energizing that the group asked to come together again. In fact, following the second meeting, the consensus was to meet weekly until a communication plan had been developed. The group realized the importance of a cohesive approach to parish communications. Their discussions included reflection on the U.S. bishops' pastoral letter on evangelization, followed by evaluation of the many ways in which the parish communicates with parishioners: the bulletin, e-mail, Web site, postal mail, homily/Mass announcements, posters, and so on. To date, the parish's logo has been updated, mailings are more effective, and their Web site is being re-designed. They have done all this with a sense of gratitude that the parish has found ways to use their gifts and talents.

How will parishioners know what is happening through parishioner-led ministries? One of the most baffling areas of stewardship ministry is keeping up-to-date with what ministries are doing and how ministries are growing. Without this information, it is difficult to put a face on parish stewardship for parishioners, to help them see the impact of people's involvement, and to understand the impact of stewardship in people's lives (both those who are serving and those being served). Some means of ongoing communication from the ministries to the stewardship commission or staff liaison needs to be established. It doesn't have to be anything too extensive, just something that helps to keep people in touch. A regular system for communication also helps the pastoral council, staff liaison, or pastor to get up-to-date information to members. Often those involved in ministry are the first people who need to know about developments in the parish's life in a timely manner. Having a communication structure already in place will help in such instances.

Practice Four: Coordination

How will ministry coordinators get help or find new members when needed? Most parish ministries are capably led by parishioners who, following a period of formation, need only occasional support. Often questions can be answered quickly over the phone, and coordinators are happy and thrive with just a periodic check-in. Those who stay connected to ministry coordinators need to keep the big picture of parish life well in mind, either through a parish group such as the stewardship commission or through regular conversation with a pastoral staff member.

Recently, a small group of stewardship commission members offered to help their parish "connect the dots." These dot-connectors are all people who have been deeply involved in stewardship ministry for many years. They know the many ways in which the parish is living as a "good steward," and they understand the challenges of the ministry coordinator since each has facilitated at least one parish ministry in the past. The connect-the-dots members have taken responsibility to be the connecting point for a group of ministries. Each ministry coordinator will receive a call at least three times a year for a brief check-in and updating of the parish's records, with longer conversations taking place as needed.

Practice Five: Collaboration

How can parish leaders discern when new ministries are called for or when existing ministries are no longer needed? Parishioner-led ministries begin through discernment that service is needed, either within the parish or for the needs of people beyond the parish. The process of discernment to consider a possible new ministry or whether a ministry is still needed can be quite simple, and if it is designed in advance, it can be adjusted to suit specific gatherings of parishioner leaders.

A definite structure for the development, coordination, and support of ministries is essential. At first, things may simply develop from the ministries that are already a part of the parish's life, but at some point, it is likely that some centralized coordination will begin to take place, either by way of a parishioner team (which could be a sub-group of the stewardship commission) or a pastoral staff member or both. Larger parishes will likely find a varied approach to be most helpful while smaller parishes may find that a parishioner team is able to coordinate the details in beneficial ways.

» What is your experience within your own parish?

» What practices are you aware of that contribute to people fully participating in the life of your parish?

» What ideas do you have for ways to build upon what is already taking place within your parish, or for developing new practices to enhance participation?

PRINCIPLE 5

Discipleship and Stewardship

"Well done, good and trustworthy slave; you have been trustworthy in a few things, I will put you in charge of many things; enter into the joy of your master."
~MATTHEW 25:21

Challenge parishioners to live gospel values as *disciples* of Jesus Christ and *stewards* of all they are, have, and will be. This is principle number five.

Therese was invited to give a stewardship witness before Mass last spring. Here is what she shared:

> While I grew up in a family that knew and lived stewardship in many ways, we never would have used that word. My mother simply taught stewardship by example, offering more of herself and my family's resources than what I thought wise. I did not really begin to reflect on myself as a steward until about ten years ago.
>
> By that time, my husband and children and I were settled into a fairly simple routine that included my involvement in the choir and my husband's as an RCIA sponsor. Then I began to sense that God might

be calling me to re-focus, and with that came striking conversations with friends and colleagues, each of whom in one way or another encouraged me to follow the promptings of my heart. In one important moment, a friend commented, "You know if you could ever really let go and trust in God, you'd find that it can be a lot of fun!" and that comment changed my life. My friend was right, and what has followed has been grace upon grace.

I began to tease about that "trust thing" as I became more willing to rely upon God to provide what our family needed, and to be convinced that God would walk with me throughout this journey of life. Not long after that conversation with my friend, my husband came home from Commitment Sunday Mass, deeply moved. He had recently declined an invitation to a new ministry, and he began to see that he really did have the gifts needed to serve in that way. His decision to step out in faith, and mine to learn to trust, have had lasting impact on our family. It hasn't always been easy. It is necessary at times to sacrifice, but then we recall that many saw how Jesus sacrificed and thought he wasn't wise for doing so. We are the recipients of his sacrifice, and as we follow him, we learn to give in many ways ourselves.

Our family has had to consider what is really important. We had to learn to budget our time carefully. We had already budgeted our money carefully, but a few years ago we began to ask ourselves how much we really needed and how much we simply wanted. And, we began to budget the ways in which we offer the talents we've been given, finding that the more we offer and the more we grow, the more God's joy fills our hearts. As a family we've been stretched and pulled, and there have been times when we've questioned God's wisdom in all of this. We are learning to trust God in big and small ways, though, as individuals and as a family. What we have found is very simple: "All we are, and all we have, and all we'll ever be is God's." We are simply stewards of those many gifts. The things we have often taken most for granted turned out to be gifts God gave us that we just needed to share with others. We've been blessed beyond abundance, with simple things to offer and simple things to receive. And we have learned that what we really need to do is to grow in gratitude and generosity, to be willing to sacrifice and to trust. God will take care of the rest, and it really can be a lot of fun!

Therese's witness is testimony to the ongoing transformation of one who is embracing stewardship as the way of living as a Christian disciple.

Becoming a disciple of Jesus Christ leads naturally to the practice of stewardship. These linked realities, discipleship and stewardship, then make up the fabric of a Christian life in which each day is lived in an intimate, personal relationship with the Lord. Refracted through the prisms of countless individual vocations, this way of life embodies and expresses the one mission of Christ: to do God's will, to proclaim the Good News of salvation, to heal the afflicted, to care for one's sisters and brothers, to give life—life to the full— as Jesus did. Following Jesus is the work of a lifetime. At every step forward, one is challenged to go further in accepting and loving God's will. (*Stewardship: A Disciple's Response*, p. 14)

Discipleship and Stewardship

A **disciple** is one who is learning what it means to live his or her faith in Christ fully. As humans, our life as disciples is sure to include failing from time to time; we're not perfect! We rely on the grace of God (often, thank God, experienced through the sacramental life of the Church) to strengthen us as we walk the journey of discipleship. "Following Jesus is the work of a lifetime. At every step forward, one is challenged to go further in accepting and loving God's will. Being a disciple is not just something else to do, alongside many other things suitable for Christians; it is a total way of life and requires continuing conversion."

(Stewardship: A Disciple's Response, p. 15)

Stewards are those who understand that all they are, have, and will be is from God and they share their lives with others in response. "What, then, are Christians to do? Of course people's lives as stewards take countless forms, according to their unique vocations and circumstances. Still, the fundamental pattern in every case is simple and changeless: 'Serve one another through love...bear one another's burdens, and so you will fulfill the law of Christ'" (Gal 5:13, 6:2).

(Stewardship: A Disciple's Response, p. 40)

THE COMMUNITY OF BELIEVERS

When we begin to see the parish as a community of believers who are mutually dependent and who challenge each other to embrace discipleship, the real meaning of stewardship begins to come alive. There has been much temptation in the past to apply stewardship too narrowly, only to the financial aspects of parish life, and often only at the time of the annual parish financial appeal. Stewardship, however, is the result of that real relationship with Christ that results in powerful living discipleship, and as such it has consequences in the totality of our lives. How can we embrace living discipleship and stewardship as individuals and as a whole community?

The decision to live as a community that embraces stewardship as a way of life typically does not happen all at once. Often the decision follows a period of challenge for the parish; quite often a financial challenge prompts the initial exploration of stewardship. When the pastor and pastoral leaders reach a decision to foster stewardship within the parish, they are taking a step of faith that truly has the power to change the life of the community and the lives of individuals. It is in many ways how the life of the disciple becomes "real," as people begin to think about their priorities, about how they spend their time, give of their financial resources, and see themselves as created and gifted by God for the building up of God's reign.

> Think of your own experience. When have you experienced a realization of your own journey as a disciple and steward? Who or what helped you to grow from that experience?

THE MEANING OF STEWARDSHIP

Beginning conversations about stewardship are often as much about dispelling inaccurate or incomplete notions of the concept as about building an understanding of what being a steward is. In some parishes, "stewardship" is still only used to describe action that takes place within or for the parish, while the truth of the concept is that it is, as our bishops remind us in their pastoral letter quoted above, a way of life, in all of one's life.

Often it seems that pastoral leaders who begin to consider stewardship in the parish seek a quick fix, a "program" that can be employed in a year with lasting results. Our hearts tell us, of course, that anything that will have lasting results will take time to establish and will need consistent attention. Fostering stewardship as a way of life will take a commitment to continue growth over time.

Embracing the life of the steward requires a leap of faith for the individual and for the parish community. As Therese described, no longer do we just talk about following Christ. Now the details of daily life are evaluated based on our faith and our desire to look to Jesus as our model for living. The steward walks the walk, even when doing so calls us to sacrifice.

EMBRACING STEWARDSHIP

This, more than most other areas of parish life, will take the time and energy of many. Moving toward stewardship as a parish priority will require the commitment of the pastor, who will work in close collaboration with parishioner leaders. Most parishes that are beginning the stewardship journey will form a stewardship commission or committee comprised of parishioners and the pastor, sometimes with a pastoral staff member as liaison. This parishioner group makes recommendations to the pastor and parish pastoral council, directing the ways in which stewardship will be lived within the parish. The group will become an essential guiding force as the parish's stewardship efforts begin to take shape. Because stewardship touches upon every facet of life for individuals and the community, the stewardship commission will need to work closely with parishioners and pastoral staff who direct or minister in all other facets of the parish.

The parish that has decided to walk the path of stewardship as a community will need to first form its leaders. This often takes the form of reflection on the U.S. bishops' pastoral letter, with opportunities for the leaders to recognize the ways in which they are already living as stewards. The realization that many of us are already on the path of stewardship is very helpful. Sometimes at the beginning people will look at stewardship as some other new expectation, something else we are supposed to "do." It is wonderful to recognize the ways in which we are already living as stewards and to realize that we have patterns in our lives upon which to build.

Because stewardship is so intimately linked to discipleship, forming people as stewards will be one thread of the fabric of faith formation for all in the parish, and all parish communication and practices will need to be consistent with the desire for parishioners and for the parish to be good stewards. This is one of the reasons that making the decision to foster stewardship is not to be taken lightly. It is also one of the greatest benefits for parishioners and for the parish, since the consistency of approach that results from parishioner leaders and groups working together helps to provide the support and the challenge necessary for stewardship to become a way of life.

DEVELOPING A VISION

"Well done, good and trustworthy slave; you have been trustworthy in a few things, I will put you in charge

of many things; enter into the joy of your master."
~Matthew 25:21

Two of the slaves in the parable of the talents were rewarded for their use of what was given. The other slave, the one who hid the talent, was punished,

> You wicked and lazy slave! You knew, did you, that I reap where I did not sow and gather where I did not scatter? Then you ought to have invested my money with the bankers and on my return I would have received what was my own with interest. So take the talent from him, and give it to the one with the ten talents. For to all those who have, more will be given, and they will have an abundance, but from those who have nothing, even what they have will be taken away. As for this worthless slave, throw him into the outer darkness, where there will be weeping and gnashing of teeth. (Matthew 25:26)

While the talent of which Jesus spoke was a form of money, there is an obvious parallel to how God wants us not only to use our talents but to give them back with increase. Jesus, of course, is the master and not only rewards us for using our talents but shows us how they grow when we use them. Good disciples know that they are using their talents for the good of God and for the fulfillment of God's mission. Are there talents in your parish that are being buried instead of invested?

What the Documents Say

In addition to the bishops' pastoral letter on stewardship, there are numerous resources from our Church teachings that reinforce and expand our challenge to be disciples and stewards. The name alone indicates the need for discipleship; *Go and Make Disciples* is the U.S. bishops' document on evangelization. Notice the title indicates the active: "Go and Make." This 2001 work followed Pope John Paul II's call for a new evangelization in 1983. This in turn renewed Pope Paul VI's 1975 apostolic exhortation, *Evangelii Nuntiandi* (On Evangelization in the Modern World) in which he said:

And may the world of our time, which is searching, sometimes with anguish, sometimes with hope, be enabled to receive the Good News not from evangelizers who are dejected, discouraged, impatient, or anxious, but from ministers of the gospel whose lives glow with fervor, who have first received the joy of Christ, and who are willing to risk their lives so that the kingdom may be proclaimed and the Church established in the midst of the world. (#80)

Go and Make Disciples, written twenty-five years after *Evangelii Nuntiandi*, sets goals for evangelization. The reasons are many, but one stands out as uniquely connected to stewardship:

Finally, the Lord gave us yet another reason to evangelize: our love for every person, whatever his or her situation, language, physical, mental, or social condition. Because we have experienced the love of Christ, we want to share it. The gifts God has given to us are not gifts for ourselves....Like the large catch of fish or the overflowing measure of flour, faith makes our hearts abound with a love-filled desire to bring all people to Jesus' gospel and to the table of the Eucharist. As Jesus wanted to gather all Jerusalem, "as a hen gathers her young," so also do we want to gather all people into God's kingdom, proclaiming the gospel even "to the ends of the earth." (p. 19)

Later, it echoes *Evangelii Nuntiandi*'s call for passionate ministers: "When the story of Jesus is truly our story, when we have caught his fire, when his Good News shapes our lives individually, as families and households, and as a Church, his influence will be felt far beyond our church" (*Go and Make Disciples*, p. 31). The movement from discipleship toward stewardship is put in motion.

Thus this connection of evangelization and discipleship leads to stewardship. For those already evangelized, such as youth and young adults involved in church activity, the bishops also address discipleship and stewardship. *Renewing the Vision* says that "The Church's ministry with adolescents seeks to...cultivate the gifts and talents of young people, and empower them to utilize these gifts and talents in leadership and ministry in the Church and community including peer ministry and intergenerational skills" (p. 17). Furthermore, one of the components of youth ministry, Leadership Development, "calls forth, affirms and empowers the diverse gifts, talents, and abilities of adults and young people in our faith communities" (p. 40). Likewise, in *Sons and Daughters of the Light*, the bishops define discipleship: "For young adults, as for all Catholic adults, the Catholic faith is lived in the "ordinary dynamics of life—caring for a family, job responsibilities, exercising duties of citizenship" (p. 22).

This is what discipleship is all about. The world is the place where men and women fulfill their Christian vocation. The mission of the Church is not directed at itself, but at nurturing and forming people who "are called by God so that they, led by the spirit of the Gospel, might contribute to the sanctification of the world, as from within like leaven, by fulfilling their own particular duties. Through the call to holiness, community, and service, the whole Church provides the necessary support for young adults to be disciples of Christ living their faith, nourished by the Church and proclaiming with the prophets of old: 'The spirit of the Lord is upon me, because he has anointed me to bring glad tidings to the poor. He has sent me to proclaim liberty to captives and recovery of sight to the blind, to let the oppressed go free, and to proclaim a year acceptable to the Lord (Lk 4:18–19)'" (p. 22).

What vision of a parish of disciples and stewards emerges for you from these documents? If you were asked to describe this vision in one sentence, what would you say?

Exploring Successful Practice

Practice One: Formation Takes Many Forms

Stewardship formation may take many forms and is most successful when it takes place throughout the year, building season upon season, providing for parishioners' reflection and growth over time. Sometimes the word "stewardship" won't be used, but the message conveys stewardship nonetheless. This is particularly helpful if the word has been used in the past only to speak of financial giving.

Some stewardship formation materials can be communicated in writing. These include mailings that are sent throughout the year or stewardship pieces that are included in other all-parish mailings; an annual stewardship renewal piece that includes stewardship formation along with the means for parishioners to make their stewardship commitment in all facets of their lives; an ongoing column in the parish bulletin and parish newsletter. It is tremendously helpful to invite parishioners with writing or design skills to become involved in the development of parish stewardship pieces. There is great benefit to communicating the ways in which stewardship is connected to our faith in Christ and to everyday living. Stewardship becomes the place where faith and real life meet, where discipleship gets its "skin." Writing in a way that enhances these connections will greatly benefit parishioners and the parish's stewardship efforts.

Some stewardship formation will be verbal. Homilists or lay witnesses can talk about how their faith has led them to re-align priorities in their lives. A yearly stewardship summary can become part of the annual parish rhythm (this summary includes growth in ministry, numbers of people involved in ministry, how people have been served, and a financial overview of the past year). There can be an annual gathering to celebrate the many ways people are living as stewards or to recognize the contributions of long-standing members.

Some stewardship formation is active. Intergenerational or adult faith formation gatherings with a discipleship or stewardship focus offer parishioners an extended time to focus on a particular facet of stewardship. An annual ministry fair can give parishioners a way of discerning what parish ministries need their involvement and is also a wonderful testimony to the ways in which stewardship is being lived. Mini-ministry fairs, with displays in the back of church and recognition of ministries during Mass, help parishioners see that ordinary people are doing wonderful things as disciples of the Lord.

At a recent stewardship formation evening in one parish, participants of all ages began together with prayer and a brief introduction before the children were taken to age-group activities. The adults shared reflections in small groups on the introduction of *Stewardship: A Disciple's Response*, followed by large-group sharing. The participants began speaking about the ways in which their lives are changing as a result of being stewards, and a few discussed the challenges of finding a good fit in ministry or service, given their family and work demands. One parishioner commented, "For a long while I thought that stewardship was something that was only about the parish. Then, one day, listening to a friend who used 'stewardship' as a way of describing the time she and her family commit to taking care of an elderly neighbor, stewardship became something totally different for me. I suddenly saw it as a way of giving myself to others: my family, my neighbors, my world, and then I understood that my parish will help me learn to do this better and more fully."

We've already spoken of the ways in which lay witnesses can provide insight into and encouragement for people on the journey of faith. Almost always when a parishioner provides a witness before Mass, part of the focus of the witness is about how embracing stewardship has changed him or her. In just three or four minutes, a well-crafted witness can convey a heartfelt message of the power of an authentic relationship with Christ and of living out one's faith as a disciple and steward.

When people see their parish as a collection of disciples who help one another, encourage one another, and challenge one another to live as followers of Jesus Christ, the lives of individuals are transformed and so is the community!

Practice Two: Gratitude and Generosity

Developing an "attitude of gratitude" will fundamentally change us, and forming a parish community that has this attitude as its foundation will fundamentally shift the ways in which we view parish. Becky, a parishioner in a parish that is fostering stewardship, recently commented on this. She said she often hears people expressing their gratitude for something that another person has done, and she thinks she should get in the habit of sharing that kind of good "gossip." Because we are so interrelated, she said, though we may not see the person to whom we are grateful, we can see the impact of something they did, and we express our gratitude to others. "Can you imagine what that person did?" we might say, or "How wonderful!" So, Becky said, she has decided to spread "gratitude gossip" as often as she is able. Another parishioner, Jack, recently offered an additional suggestion. In our general intercessions, Jack commented, wouldn't it be wonderful to offer a prayer of thanksgiving: "We give thanks this day for the women and men who serve those who grieve. May their ministry continue to reach out to those who are sorrowing, we pray to the Lord."

Forming individuals and our communities in the ways of gratitude leads us to be people who recognize that everything we are and have comes from God. Sometimes generosity flows in direct proportion to gratitude. When that happens, the pastoral leader's role is to help direct the outpouring of resources, matching gifts with recipients. For example, it is not uncommon for people to volunteer for familiar ministries when other less visible ministries continue to need volunteers. Bringing the work of the understaffed groups to the awareness of those who are ready to serve is often enough to encourage their participation.

At times generosity flows from relationships. Many parishioners become more generous when the parish is committed in relationship with a community in need, whether in an impoverished area of the U.S. or a community in need elsewhere in the world. The relationships that form and the examples of gratitude and generosity in the face of great poverty are often inspiring and spark increased generosity among parishioners.

Nothing brings the Eucharist home like a conversation about gratitude. In catechetical gatherings and homilies, bulletin letters and parish meetings, the subject of gratitude emerges as one that has particular meaning for today's Catholics. Often the conversations begin when we explain that the word "Eucharist" means "thanksgiving." Rather than coming to "get" something (communion, for example, or the weekly readings, or the homily, or the companionship of others), what we really come to do is "give" something: our gratitude. And if giving gratitude is an essential aspect of Eucharist, it must necessarily be part of our lives at other times as well.

Practice Three: A Covenant

Many parishes that embrace stewardship as a way of life have an annual renewal period that includes a commitment process for the members in their households. The renewal period often includes homilies that highlight the connections between the gospel and stewardship; lay witnesses at Masses; parish ministry and financial reports; a ministry fair; and something to encourage households and individuals to reflect on the ways in which they are living and growing as stewards in all facets of their lives. Parishioners are then invited to make a commitment to the ways in which they will live as stewards in the coming year.

Parishes have found that a covenanting process is particularly beneficial, as a challenge to embrace discipleship as a lifelong pattern of conversion. The covenant includes a commitment to the ways in which each person or household will offer themselves as Christian stewards throughout the coming year. A statement of commitment is signed and brought forward after the homily on Commitment Sunday. In some parishes, the statements are later signed by the pastor and pastoral council chairperson as a sign and witness of the ways in which parishioners and the parish, as the body of Christ acting in unity, will live as disciples and stewards in the coming year. A copy of the signed covenant is then mailed to the households as a reminder of their commitment to stewardship.

Some communities hold a covenanting celebration in which members are invited to report on how they have lived and grown as stewards in the previous year. In some parishes, the bulletin or a special insert includes examples of how parishioners are offering themselves in service to others. Some communities include opportunities for parishioners to discern ways in which they will grow as stewards in the coming year, and then participants complete their covenant at the end of the gathering. In all of these ways, parishes help their members to understand that stewardship is not just about the parish; stewardship is the disciple's way, in all of their lives, including their life within the parish community. For additional examples of the covenant process, go to our Web site, www. thegenerousheart.com.

» What is your experience within your parish?

» What practices are you aware of that contribute to living discipleship?

» What ideas do you have for ways to build upon what is already taking place within your parish, or for developing new practices to enhance stewardship?

Meaningful Service

"So if I, your Lord and Teacher, have washed your feet, you also ought to wash one another's feet. For I have set you an example, that you also should do as I have done to you." ~JOHN 13:14–15

Become a parish in which every person is invited, encouraged, and expected to offer *meaningful service* within the parish and in their lives, and which acknowledges the ways in which ministry is given. This is principle number six.

Dee and Jack have been part of their parish for over thirty years. As time has passed, they have served in many ways, offering their gifts as they were able at different stages of their lives. Dee would be quick to say, however, that the giving is for a reason: "When others give, they remind me of the ways God is generous with me. I figure I can be that kind of reminder to other people—in really simple ways. When our bereavement hospitality group offers a meal to follow a funeral, we're setting the stage for memories to be shared, healing to take place, love to be felt. It takes a bit of organizing, because we only have a few days to get the pieces in place after someone dies. It seems a small thing to offer people, but I know that it really makes a difference in their lives. We are told over and over again how powerfully people experience God's love through a funeral celebration at the parish."

Early in an individual's relationship with the faith community, the person begins to ask the question "what should I give?" Later, he or she is ready to take the next step toward true belonging by looking at the opportunities the parish provides for offering meaningful service, based in the unique gifts each person possesses (Winseman, p. 82–83). Belonging to and becoming engaged in a community of disciples will encourage us to give generously to our parish and to those in need in our city and world.

Think of your own experience. When have you offered or invited someone else to offer service in a meaningful way? Who or what helped you to grow from that experience?

Becoming a parish in which each person is given the opportunity to offer meaningful service requires commitment in many ways. The shift that takes place when people are invited to discern ministries that are needed and ways to provide ministry within the community is profound. The impact in people's lives is even more profound. Serving and being served is part of being community, a family of faith, and as Dee's comments remind us, it is often in the act of giving and receiving service that we recognize God's love.

AN ILLUSTRATION

Picture a gymnasium overflowing with hand-me-down "stuff." Tables have been set up in a loosely organized

Response to God's Call

Serving is simply part of the life of the disciple, a way of answering God's call to faith in Christ. "Jesus' call is urgent. He does not tell people to follow him at some time in the future but here and now—at this moment, in these circumstances. There can be no delay. 'Go and proclaim the kingdom of God....No one who sets a hand to the plow and then looks to what was left behind is fit for the kingdom of God.'"

(Stewardship: A Disciple's Response, p. 14)

fashion, and there are people of all ages working at a quick pace. Young children accompany parents or teens in carrying items to specified areas. Teens and adults carry furniture, exercise equipment, and baby strollers to the cafeteria and a designated hallway. This is the scene every year for the annual garage sale to benefit the parish's twinning community. Two couples first came up with the idea after they visited the twinning community. Now the sale raises nearly $15,000 each year, with hundreds of parishioners giving time to collect and organize donations, set up the sale the evening before, sell the items on the day of the sale, and clean up afterward. It is inspiring to see young children learning how to serve side-by-side with their parents and siblings. Walking through as the sale is being set up, one can hear parents explaining the importance of the sale to their children and attesting to the need for the materials the sale will fund.

GROWING AS DISCIPLES

The garage sale is one example of the ways in which young children learn to offer meaningful service. Catechesis and companionship are the ways of stewardship formation, for both children and for adults. Each person discerns the gifts he or she has been given and the ways in which those gifts can be used in service of others. Stewardship as a way of life begins with the toddler who cries, "I need that!" and whose parent replies, "No, that is something you want, not something you need." Together parent and toddler must go through the early steps of prioritization.

Formation for meaningful service continues when, for example, parish youth are asked to experience three different kinds of stewardship as part of their confirmation preparation: stewardship in the home, the community, and the parish. For each stewardship experience, the young person completes a guided reflection that includes the question: "Is this an area in which you will offer ministry again in the future?" Parishes that have been fostering stewardship for many years attest to what happens when people are given opportunities to offer themselves in service: young children eventually grow into adults who know stewardship as a way of life, plain, simple, and profound.

DEVELOPING A VISION

"So if I, your Lord and Teacher, have washed your feet, you also ought to wash one another's feet. For I have set you an example, that you also should do as I have done to you." ~JOHN 13:14–15

John's gospel includes the washing of the feet in the description of the last supper. By modeling the act typically done by a servant, Jesus connects his upcoming passion to service. It is not only John's account of the foot washing that confirms the importance of service. The synoptic gospels each account for Jesus sending the early disciples out on mission. As Jesus healed and fed others, he encouraged his followers to do the same. Service to the community is even his last command to Peter: "Feed my sheep" (John 21:17).

WHAT THE DOCUMENTS SAY

The imperative of this mission of service is found throughout church documents. The *Catechism of the Catholic Church*, says this of missionary paths:

> The Holy Spirit is the protagonist, the principal agent of the whole of the Church's mission. It is he who leads the Church on her missionary paths. This mission continues and, in the course of history, unfolds the mission of Christ, who was sent to evangelize the poor; so the Church, urged on by the Spirit of Christ, must walk the road Christ himself walked, a way of poverty and obedience, of service and self-sacrifice.... (#852)

The third goal of *Go and Make Disciples* is that of fostering values in society: "Our faith must touch the values of the United States" (p. 65). Here catechesis is an important partner in forming meaningful service: "Catechesis shall arouse in catechumens and those receiving catechesis 'a preferential option for the poor....' This option is not exclusive but implies a commitment to justice, according to each individual's role, vocation and circumstances" (*Catechism of the Catholic Church*, #104). The themes of Catholic social teaching are starting points for effective engagement and education in social justice. They are: 1)

Life and Dignity of the Human Person, 2) Call to Family, 3) Community and Participation, 4) Rights and Responsibilities, 5) Option for the Poor and Vulnerable, 6) The Dignity of Work and the Rights of Workers, 7) Solidarity and Care for God's Creation. As people—young and old—participate in meaningful service, these seven themes should be revisited. *Renewing the Vision* reminds us of the importance of helping young people recognize that the Catholic faith calls them to work for justice and to defend human dignity (p. 16–17). This awareness is not only important for youth, but for each one of us. Regarding catechesis in general, the *National Directory for Catechesis* states, "Those responsible for catechesis (are required) to give greater attention to providing catechesis that…gives greater attention to the social teachings of the Church" (p. 13–14).

What vision of a parish of meaningful service emerges for you from these documents? If you were asked to describe this vision in one sentence, what would you say?

EXPLORING SUCCESSFUL PRACTICE

Practice One: Discover and Develop Gifts

Growing as disciples and stewards leads us to desire to *discern our gifts* in order to be able to more authentically offer those gifts in service. It is not uncommon to hear people say, "I know I should be giving my talents back to

God, but I'm not sure I know what my talents are." Some will say they understand how to use their gifts and skills at home or in the workplace, but they're less sure in other contexts, especially those who have not previously offered themselves in service. In fact, it is the failure to identify one's talents that is a primary obstacle for many who are ready to offer service within the parish or in their community. Think of what it was like for you when you first began: someone likely invited you and others probably explained the mission of the group, how the group functioned, and described the expectations or needs of new members. For long-time parishioners who have never become involved, being invited and mentored is as essential to the process as knowing their talents and how to apply them.

Nowhere else in this book do we directly point you to a specific resource, although many are listed in the end to help you as you begin or continue this journey with your parish. Where talent-identification is concerned, however, one unique process stands out as being particularly important, both from the standpoint of what it provides individuals, and in terms of the benefit to the parish community. *Living Your Strengths* (order information is found in the resource section) includes an online assessment called the "Clifton StrengthsFinder," a thirty-minute survey that parishioners complete on their own. Dr. Donald Clifton, the primary influence in the development of the StrengthsFinder, discovered through extensive research over a span of thirty years that people possess thirty-four themes of talent or strength, in one degree or another. When an individual completes StrengthsFinder, the computer rank-orders the person's strengths, providing the person with the list of their Top 5 Signature Themes. *Living Your Strengths* then provides the person with descriptions of his or her strengths, passages of scripture with which to pray, life connections to consider, and examples of application in ministry or service. Within the insights the individual acquires, two statistics will stand out: we have a 1 in 275,000 chance of meeting someone with our same Top 5 in the course of our lifetime, and a 1 in 33 million chance of meeting someone with our same Top 5 in the same order. We are, indeed, uniquely and wonderfully created, with a purpose that is unique to each person!

Remember earlier we spoke of how there is a much higher rate of engagement in those who say they can do what they do best in their parish community? The increase in engagement in parishes that use *Living Your Strengths* as the basis for talent-identification and subsequent ministry development and/or discernment is decidedly marked. Parishioners value the process, not just for its connection to parish ministry, but because of the insights they discover for the whole of their lives. Young adults find it helpful as they are experiencing their first experiences of work and deepening relationships. Couples find beneficial insights for their married relationships, and conversations at the dinner tables in households are strengthened.

Practice Two: Discernment

The annual stewardship renewal period is a good time for people to be reminded to take stock of their lives in light of their faith. An examination of the ways in which God has blessed individuals or families and the ways in which people are responding to those blessings in prayer, action, awareness, and presence is a powerful way to encourage growth in stewardship. Because we are so surrounded with messages that lead us to believe we're "entitled," it is important to counter those subtle messages with reminders of the ways in which we experience God's grace in our lives. An annual stewardship "check-up" is a great way to stay in shape as a good steward. Questions for this check-up might include: How is God's grace present in your life? How is God blessing you? How are you responding? How are you taking responsibility for the ways in which you live your life? In what ways are you going beyond yourself in service? How have you experienced God's presence as you served others this year? In what ways will you challenge yourself this coming year to reach out to someone in need? How are you offering yourself in generous response to the lavish gift of Christ's love? (For resources to help parishioners discern the ways in which they will offer themselves as stewards, go to our Web site at www.thegenerousheart.com.)

Following this period of self-examination, parishioners may be invited to submit their reflections to the stewardship commission, a pastoral staff member, an idea-box in the vestibule of church, or a parishioner-mentor. In one parish, people are paired with parishioner-mentors who contact them at least twice a year. The purpose of the contact is simply to offer spiritual support and to ask if help is needed in matching people with appropriate ministries. The result of this kind of mentoring is immeasurable.

Some parishes develop a ministry of Gifts Coordinator, parishioners who meet one-on-one or in small groups with those ready to discern a good ministry fit. The Gifts Coordinators have up-to-date information about ministry needs and lead the parishioners through a process that helps them celebrate the talents they bring to a ministerial setting. Together the Gifts Coordinator and parishioner discern the ministry that could most benefit from the parishioner's service to the community.

Practice Three: Feature Ministry Opportunities

Ministry Fair: Most parishes that are serious about stewardship as a way of life will hold an annual ministry fair. Not only is the fair an opportunity for people to hear about ministries, it can also be a yearly celebration of all that happens as a result of the selfless service of parishioners. Invite parish musicians to offer their gifts in providing entertainment. Offer refreshments, include games, balloons, video presentations of ministries in action, and the stage has been set for a weekend of fun and friendship.

Ministry Guidebook: Publish a booklet that includes descriptions of the ministries in which people may become involved in the parish. Include contact information for the coordinator of each ministry and particular gifts or talents that are helpful for it.

Hospitality Sundays: These are mini-ministry fairs with an emphasis on one aspect of parish life. They are often held once a month or quarterly in the back of church or in the parish hall after Masses. One month might feature outreach to the poor or those in crisis. The next event might feature opportunities to become involved in liturgical ministries, and so on. Hospitality Sundays may simply feature those ministries that have a new or different need for parishioner involvement.

Practice Four: Be Thankful

"Thank you!" goes a long way. Nothing flashy is needed, just an occasional and simple "thank you" will help people who are offering ministry to know that their service is important and that they are valued. The gratitude may be expressed in the parish bulletin and verbal acknowledgment is also wonderful when possible.

Each year, some pastors send a thank-you postcard to every parishioner who is involved in ministry in the parish. The cards arrive in people's homes just a few days before Thanksgiving. Typically the card has a photo of the church on one side, with a brief two-sentence note on the reverse. This is such a simple sign of the parish's gratitude, but it speaks volumes. People will say repeatedly that they don't want the parish spending lots of money for gratitude gifts—they would rather the money be given to those who truly need it—but a brief note expressing gratitude is more than sufficient.

» What is your experience within your parish?

» What practices are you aware of that contribute to people feeling they are invited and encouraged to offer meaningful service?

» What ideas do you have for ways to build upon what is already taking place for developing new practices to enhance a sense of service?

PRINCIPLE 7

Caring Community

"Day by day, as they spent much time together in the temple, they broke bread at home, and ate their food with glad and generous hearts, praising God and having the goodwill of all the people." ~ACTS 2:46–47

Create a community in which parishioners *care* for one another and for those in need in the community and the world. This is principle number seven.

A few years ago, one of the parish's young teens became suddenly ill and was rushed to intensive care. She is one of a trio of triplets. Amy and her siblings were part of the parish's religious education program, and her mother was a middle-school catechist.

At that time, the families whose children attended public schools seemed to stay on the margins of parish life. It was not uncommon to hear the religious education families speak of being "second-class citizens" and expressing the belief that the parish did not care about them. Over the years, however, the climate changed in the parish, as families came together to experience sacramental preparation, intergenerational catechesis, and community events. Most of the religious education families are now actively living discipleship in wonderful ways, fully participating in parish life, and generously serving the poor in their city and world. They would be the first to tell you their lives have changed.

So, as Amy and her family struggled through those first long days (Amy had an aneurism, and was at one point so near death that the doctors were beginning to prepare the family for the task of taking her off life support), the community began to rally around them. By mid-week, one of the religious education parents called the pastor and asked about a Mass of healing. The pastor suggested that the families gather for the regular Saturday morning liturgy, and offer that Mass in a particular way for Amy and all who were seriously ill. Phone trees were put into place; paper balloons and flowers were cut out for people to write messages to Amy and her family, and green ribbons were cut for people to wear as a sign of hope.

Amazingly, five hundred people gathered on that Saturday morning, surrounding Amy's family with love and care and prayer. Even the high school football team arrived, complete with neckties, to be with the community that morning. It did not occur to those people to talk of what the parish "should" do. They know now that they are the parish, and they know that the community should gather, and would want to gather, to pray with and for Amy and her family.

Miraculously, Amy lived, and she continues to receive the love and care of the parish family through the long and difficult hours of rehabilitation and in the more common, everyday moments of life. She and her family and all of the five hundred who were there that Saturday morning continue to walk the journey of caring discipleship together. Many of the parishioners who reached out to

Amy and her family did not know them before Amy's illness. Many had never considered the support that those who have a child in the hospital need; some had never reached out beyond themselves before this experience, but being part of the community drew them beyond themselves, and they now serve in ways that would have been beyond their imagination just a few years ago.

The fruit of evangelization is changed lives and a changed world—holiness and justice, spirituality and peace. The validity of our having accepted the gospel does not only come from what we feel or what we know; it comes also from the way we serve others, especially the poorest, the most marginal, the most hurting, the most defenseless, the least loved. An evangelization that stays inside ourselves is not an evangelization into the Good News of Jesus Christ. (*Go and Make Disciples*, p. 3)

Think of your own experience. When have you experienced giving or receiving the care of your parish community? Who or what helped you to grow from that experience?

This final principle is obviously connected to all that we have explored thus far. Disciples and stewards follow the self-giving example of Jesus Christ by living for God and others first; the parish as a community of caring believers is the place in which people are formed to live beyond themselves in love.

DEVELOPING A VISION

"Day by day, as they spent much time together in the temple, they broke bread at home, and ate their food with glad and generous hearts, praising God and having the goodwill of all the people." ~ACTS 2:46– 47

First Jesus ascended into heaven, then Matthias was chosen to replace Judas. Then the Holy Spirit came to the gathered disciples at Pentecost. Peter led the group and reminded them of the prophecy that was being fulfilled in their presence, resulting in new people coming to Christ. Luke, the author of Acts, goes on to describe this new community.

They devoted themselves to the apostles' teaching and fellowship, to the breaking of bread and the prayers. Awe came upon everyone because many wonders and signs were being done by the apostles. All who believed were together and had all things in common; they would sell their possessions and goods and distribute the proceeds to all, as any had need. Day by day, as they spent much time together in the temple, they broke bread at home, and ate their food with glad and generous hearts, praising God and having the goodwill of all the people. And day by day the Lord added to their number those who were being saved. (Acts 2:42–47)

The four actions of the new community described here and at the beginning of this book are significant. They prayed and shared the sacred meal, learned together, shared their love of God, and spent time as a community. The actions aren't complicated, yet they speak of profound realities. They are just the simple acts of a community of faith. The early church community is an example of what faith communities here-and-now can be. The description in Acts is positive and cheerful. What are the primary actions of your parish community? How are you and the people of your community being formed with glad and generous hearts?

What the Documents Say

"Keep this in mind: Pentecost happened at a meeting! One of the central events that shaped Christian history did not happen to an individual off praying alone or to a monk on a mountaintop or to a solitary Buddha meditating under a tree. None of these. Pentecost occurred at a meeting of a community, to a gathering assembled for prayer waiting for God's guidance" (*Ministry through the Lens of Evangelization,* USCCB, 2004, p. 128). Spiritual writer Ronald Rolheiser says that one way to develop an evangelizing spirituality is to continue to go to church meetings because "we are waiting for God to do something in us and through us that we can't do all by ourselves: namely, create community with each other and bring justice, love, peace, and joy to our world." We are waiting and wanting to be part of community and even though we may tire of meetings, it is in the gathering that "community" happens.

Go and Make Disciples explains, "Yet our relationship with Jesus is found in our relationship with the community of Jesus—the Church. The way to Christ is through the community in which he lives" (p. 26).

Likewise, the *General Directory for Catechesis* and the *National Directory for Catechesis* both affirm the importance of the Christian Community. "The Christian community is the origin, locus, and goal of catechesis" (*General Directory for Catechesis,* 254). The principles of

Consider the quotes above: What vision of a caring community emerges for you in these documents? If you were asked to describe this vision in one sentence, what would you say?

Sons and Daughters of the Light and *Renewing the Vision* include the formation of community, not a community of adolescents and a community of young adults, but an intergenerational, diverse community. Meetings gather us and help create community. Once community is formed, the day-by-day gatherings begin to take place, and day by day the ways in which community can take place increase.

EXPLORING SUCCESSFUL PRACTICE

Discern Needs Within the Parish

Create a parish structure that provides for ways in which ministry is guided within the parish and beyond it. Needs for ministry by parish members should be regularly sought, along with strategies to meet those needs. Are there people or groups within the parish who voice needs or the sentiment that the parish does not care for them or others? How do you listen to them, difficult as that might be? Could you invite those people to become part of the solution? Listen to their ideas; it may be a simple matter of matching already-existing ministries with parishioners, or of inviting people to come forward to meet the needs in some new way.

A large suburban parish had the reputation of being too big for folks to know one another. "It's sad," members would say, "that when there is a serious illness or death in someone's family, people turn to their other social circles for help, rather than coming to the parish." Over time, the pastor and pastoral council heard this feeling voiced enough times that they realized the perception was, indeed, reality. If someone fell ill and family members needed help, where in the parish would they turn? What about the homebound who might need transportation to Mass or to doctor's visits? Finally a woman in the parish came forward. "I've been thinking a lot about how we could start a web of care within our parish, knowing that when we care for one another, we'll be better equipped to care for those who need our love in other places. I'd like to start a ministry called Helping Hands. I'll be willing to get it started and do all of the organization. Over time, maybe someone will come forward to help with this ministry. Would that be okay?" The pastor agreed, and now, some years later, over two hundred parishioners are part of the Helping Hands ministry. No longer is there a perception that the parish is too large to care for its members. Now it is not uncommon to hear sentiments that echo the early Christian communities: "It's amazing how parishioners love one another and how that love is extended beyond the parish!"

DISCERN NEEDS BEYOND YOU

As the parishioner who began Helping Hands noted, when we take care of each other, and people experience Christ's love through the love of their faith community, they will be ready to imitate Christ as one who washes the feet of those in need. The parish that hopes to really foster discipleship and stewardship will lead its members to seek ways to serve those most in need, through active service, relationship-building, charitable giving (on the part of individuals and on the part of the parish), advocacy for justice, and work for peace. Keep the fire alive in people's hearts for such ministry by forming groups to oversee all outreach and justice activity. Invite them to advise the pastoral council when new ways to reach out have come to their attention, and fashion a structure for discerning which needs to address and how.

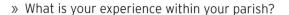

» What is your experience within your parish?

» What practices contribute to people in your parish caring for one another and for those in need?

» What ideas do you have for ways to build upon what is already taking place within your parish, or for developing new practices to enhance a sense of care within your community?

Planning with the Principles

Now it is time for you to begin to look at your parish in relationship to the principles explored in this book. For each principle, a process is provided in this chapter for reflection, discussion, and the development of a cohesive plan. The plan may become the means for addressing goals that are part of an already-existing long-range plan with strategies and practices, or it could become the basis for such a plan.

You can use the processes that follow in two ways. If there are already leadership groups (commissions, committees, or steering teams) that guide elements of your parish's life, those groups could be drawn together to study the principle most directly related to their area of responsibility, studying it as described above, bringing their recommendations to the parish Generous Hearts Team. Your team would convene all seven groups to present their conclusions and to direct the compilation of a cohesive plan.

For a more holistic approach, your Generous Hearts Team will gather input from any leadership groups already in place and from parishioners through written and/or verbal listening processes. Your team will then take time to study the principles and commit to eight meetings (one for each principle and at least one final meeting to synthesize conclusions and discern next steps), likely spread out throughout a year, in which to use the process below. A final meeting will draw together the results of the seven process meetings, with a resulting cohesive plan for your parish.

Each process begins with brief prayer and reflection on sacred scripture and an excerpt from a source related to the principle you will discuss. Questions follow to provide food for your discussion. Look at the questions in advance to determine which will be of most benefit to the work your group will undertake. It is likely that in order to discuss all of the questions in some fashion you will need to break into sub-groups for a portion of your time. The whole group would do the prayer and reflection together, and then assign a question or two to each group, leaving ample time to return to the large group for discussion and consensus concerning next steps or recommendations for the development of goals and/or action steps.

A word about consensus building or prioritization. Often discussions such as the ones that are involved with these processes will lead to a clear path for the next steps. Occasionally, as you have likely experienced, it will take some time for clarity of vision to emerge. Have newsprint and markers ready, and record all of the key insights and/or possible strategies on the newsprint. Take a few moments to stretch, and then re-gather in prayer. Invite people to express their concerns, hopes, and dreams; often roadblocks or new insights will come to light, and then consensus will build. Before the meeting ends, decide what will happen next. Will someone take responsibility for recording the newsprint notes and e-mailing them to everyone? Will the remaining work be accomplished through sub-groups or will another meeting be necessary? It is important that every participant knows that his or her thoughts have been heard and are of value; you will be able to express this value by assuring that each person has a clear understanding of what will happen next.

In addition to the newsprint and markers, if the people who are attending do not know one another, nametags will be a must! Refreshments always help to provide an atmosphere of welcome and comfort. Ask each person who will be attending to anticipate the gathering by spending a few minutes each day in prayer, and by studying the principle section to be discussed, answering the questions found within the chapter, and reflecting on their experience of the principle at your parish. You might invite participants to discuss the concepts with other parishioners in advance, or working groups could do preliminary input-gathering prior to the process.

You should plan at least two hours for each process:

Gathering and Welcome: 10 minutes

Opening Prayer and Reflection: 20 minutes

Questions for Discussion: 45 minutes

Consensus Building or Prioritization: 30 minutes

Summary and Closing Prayer: 15 minutes

PROCESS ONE: BELONGING

Facilitator: At this gathering, we will prayerfully reflect on the importance of belonging in the life of our parish. First we will listen to the words of sacred scripture and a source on evangelization. Then, we will reflect individually for a few moments, followed by group discussion. Let us first quiet our minds and hearts, and invite the Holy Spirit to guide our time together.

God of our mind, Christ of our hearts, Holy Spirit who works through our hands, we come to you as a community that seeks to be a place of welcome and belonging. As we begin this process of reflection and planning for generous hearts, let us be the first examples of them. May your guidance help us to grow as a belonging community, to be people with wide open arms that embrace our neighbors. Amen.

Reflecting on Belonging

A reading from the holy gospel according to Luke.

"Teacher," he said, "What must I do to inherit eternal life?"

He said to him, "What is written in the law? What do you read there?"

He answered, "You shall love the Lord your God with all your heart, and with all your soul, and with all your strength, and with all your mind; and your neighbor as yourself."

He said to him, "You have given the right answer; do this, and you will live. But wanting to justify himself, he asked Jesus, "And who is my neighbor?" ~LUKE 10:2–29

If the Christian mission must take its spirit and meaning from the mission of Jesus, let me cite again the fundamental image of "breathing in and breathing out." This primal human function is also a metaphor that I think describes the fundamental character of Jesus' own mission as portrayed in the gospels. I have come to think of his ministry like the work of breathing—a drawing in of life to a vital center, the extending of life to the farthest boundaries of reality, a gesture similar to an embrace, a reaching out and drawing in. The more I conceive of Jesus' mission in terms of these two related movements, the more they become one fluid action and characterize the fundamental elements of Jesus' ministry; reaching out and drawing in. Both gestures were compelled by the deepest convictions and religious instincts of his life and his vocation: reaching out in a wide embrace of the whole expanse of Israel, including those on the margins; drawing in the entire community—washed and unwashed—into a communion of life that gives glory to God. (*Ministry Through the Lens of Evangelization*, p. 142–143)

Take a few moments to reflect on the words above, first silently as individuals and then as a group.

What words or phrases strike you, particularly in light of your study of the importance of "belonging" in the life of individuals and in the life of the community?

In a few sentences, summarize what you understand about the ideas of engagement and belonging.

Questions to Guide Your Conversation

✛ What is our parish doing to encourage such a sense of engagement or belonging? Is there a perception that the parish is warm and welcoming?

✛ What practices are already in place that lead to a sense of belonging among members? Among visitors? How can we build on these to grow as a belonging community?

✛ Are there particular groups within the parish that seem to be on the margins of the faith community? What strategies could be developed to reach out to those groups in a special way?

✢ What new practices should we consider?

Following your discussion, summarize the consensus of the group with the statements below. (These statements will be used to formulate your cohesive plan after all seven principles have been studied and discussed.)

Celebrating What Is and What Will Be

Principle One: Foster a sense of belonging among all who come to the parish, and develop that sense of belonging among members throughout the moments of their lives and stages of their faith.

> » As a parish, we help people to feel they belong by...

> » As a result of our discussion, we will explore these goals, strategies, or practices...

> » The group that will be responsible for follow-up on this principle will be...

> » Their time frame for development will be...

When the summary sheet is completed, invite the group to quiet themselves in preparation for your concluding prayer.

We give thanks, O God, for your guidance during this time of reflection and planning. May the work begun here, in your name, be continued in our community. May our goals, strategies, and practices lead to a community of belonging, a place that truly lives your command to "Love your neighbor."

And we pray, "Glory be to the Father..."

As we leave this holy space, let us offer one another a sign of peace.

PROCESS TWO: LIFELONG TRANSFORMATION

Facilitator: At this gathering, we will prayerfully reflect on the importance of lifelong transformation in the life of individuals and in our parish. First we will listen to the words of sacred scripture and words from *Our Hearts Were Burning Within Us.* Then, we will reflect individually for a few moments, followed by group discussion. Let us first quiet our minds and hearts, and invite the Holy Spirit to guide our time together.

Generous God, who begins the good work in us, we come to you as a community that seeks to be a place where people of all ages continue to be transformed by you. As we enter into this process of reflection and planning, set our minds on your will, our hearts on your love, and our hands on your holy work. May your guidance help us to grow as a transformed community and help us to recognize the power of this for each of us and for our parish. Amen.

Reflecting on Transformation

A reading from the holy gospel according to John.

The next day John again was standing with two of his disciples, and as he watched Jesus walk by, he exclaimed, "Look, here is the Lamb of God!" The two disciples heard him say this, and they followed Jesus. When Jesus turned and saw them following, he said to them, "What are you looking for?" They said to him, "Rabbi" (which translated means Teacher), "where are you staying?" He said to them, "Come and see." They came and saw where he was staying, and they remained with him that day. It was about four o'clock in the afternoon. One of the two who heard John speak and followed him was Andrew, Simon

Peter's brother. He first found his brother Simon and said to him, "We have found the Messiah" (which is translated Anointed). He brought Simon to Jesus, who looked at him and said, "You are Simon son of John. You are to be called Cephas," which is translated Peter. ~John 1:35–42

God's call to conversion and discipleship unfolds in our lives with immeasurable potential for maturing and bearing fruit. The calls to holiness, to community, and to service of God and neighbor are facets of Christian life that come to full expression only by means of development and growth toward Christian maturity. This maturity of Christian faith can blossom at any age. We see it in children like Samuel who hear and respond to God's word (cf. 1 Sam 3:1–18). We see it in young people like Mary who ponder and say "yes" to God's call (cf. Lk 1:26–38). We see it in adults and marvel especially at the beauty of faith in those who have persevered in following the Lord over the full course of a lifetime: "They shall bear fruit even in old age, always vigorous and sturdy" (Ps 92:15). (*Our Hearts Were Burning Within Us*, p. 47–48)

Take a few moments to reflect on the words above, first silently as individuals, and then as a group.

What words or phrases strike you, particularly in light of your study of the importance of lifelong transformation in Christ?

In a few sentences, summarize what you understand about the importance of a lifetime of conversion to Christ.

Questions to Guide Your Conversation

✦ What is our parish doing to encourage people to

continue to grow and to be transformed in Christ throughout their lives? Do most youth and adults participate in some form of faith formation over the course of a year?

✛ What practices are already in place that support members to grow in their relationship with Christ and to live that out in powerful ways? How can we build on these to grow as a transformed community?

✛ Are there particular groups within the parish that seem not to be encouraged to embrace transformation? What strategies could be developed to reach out to these groups in a special way?

✛ What new practices should we consider?

Following your discussion, summarize the consensus of the group with the statements below. These statements will be used to formulate your cohesive plan after all seven principles have been studied and discussed.

Celebrating What Is and What Will Be

Principle Two: Experience deep conversion to Christ and create a climate in which everyone is given the opportunity to encounter and be drawn into life in Christ.

 » As a parish, we create a climate in which everyone may encounter and be drawn into life in Christ by...

 » As a result of our discussion, we will explore these goals, strategies or practices...

 » The group that will be responsible for follow-up for this principle will be...

 » Their time frame for development will be...

When the summary sheet is completed, invite the group to quiet themselves in preparation for your concluding prayer.

We give thanks, O God, for your guidance during this time of reflection and planning. May the work begun here, in your name, be continued in our community. Help us live as people with generous hearts. May our goals, strategies, and practices lead to a place of ongoing transformation, where the experiences of your love lead us to care for all your people.

And we pray, "Glory be to the Father..."

As we leave this holy space, let us offer a sign of peace to one another.

PROCESS THREE: FAITH MEETS LIFE

Facilitator: At this gathering, we will prayerfully reflect on the importance of equipping people to live their lives as disciples. First we will listen to the words of sacred scripture, and then to a theological reflection. We will reflect individually for a few moments, followed by group discussion. Let us first quiet our minds and hearts, and invite the Holy Spirit to guide our time together.

Generous God, who begins the good work in us, we come to you as a community that strives to help people bring their faith to all their life. As we begin this process of reflection and planning, set our minds on your will, our hearts on your love, and our hands on your holy work. May your guidance help us to grow as a faith-filled community with disciples willing to touch the cloak of Jesus. Amen.

Reflecting on Living Faith

A reading from the holy gospel according to Mark.

And a large crowd followed him and pressed in on him. Now there was a woman who had been suffering from hemorrhages for twelve years. She had endured much under many physicians, and had spent all that she had; and she was no better, but rather grew worse. She had heard about Jesus, and came up behind him in the crowd and touched his cloak, for she said, "If I but touch his clothes, I will be made well." Immediately her hemorrhage stopped; and she felt in her body that she was healed of her disease. Immediately aware that power had gone forth from him, Jesus turned about in the crowd and said, "Who touched my clothes?" And his disciples said to him, "You see the crowd pressing in on you; how can you say, 'Who touched me?' He looked all around to see who had done it. But the woman, knowing what had happened to her, came in fear and trembling, fell down before him, and told him the whole truth. He said to her, "Daughter, your faith has made you well; go in peace, and be healed of your disease." ~MARK 5:24B–34

The young creature in the stall of Bethlehem was a human being with a human brain and heart and soul. And it was God. Its life was to manifest the will of the Father; to proclaim the sacred tidings, to stir mankind with the power of God, to establish the Covenant, and shoulder the sin of the world, expiating it with love and leading mankind through the destruction of sacrifice and the victory of the Resurrection into the new existence of grace. In this accomplishment alone lay Jesus' self-perfection: fulfillment of mission and personal fulfillment were one. (Romano Guardini, quoted in *Stewardship, A Disciple's Response*, p. 23)

Take a few moments to reflect on the words above, first silently as individuals, and then as a group.

What words or phrases strike you, particularly in light of your study of the parish as equipping people to live their lives as disciples?

In a few sentences, summarize what you understand about the parish as a place that equips people to live their faith in everyday life.

Questions to Guide Your Conversation

✠ What is our parish doing to equip people to live their faith in their daily lives? Are there ongoing means to help people make connections between their relationship with Christ and the way they live?

✠ What practices are already in place that lead to this sort of living discipleship? How can we build on these to grow as a community of living disciples?

✠ Are there particular groups within the parish that are not challenged and encouraged to live as disciples? What strategies could be developed to reach out to those groups in a special way?

✠ What new practices should we consider?

Following your discussion, summarize the consensus of the group with the statements below. These statements will be used to formulate your cohesive plan after all seven principles have been studied and discussed.

Celebrating What Is and What Will Be

Principle Three: Faith meets life as the parish helps to equip people to live as disciples in the whole of their lives, in their home, workplace, neighborhood, and world.

» As a parish, we equip people to live as disciples in the whole of their lives by...

» As a result of our discussion, we will explore these goals, strategies, or practices...

» The group that will be responsible for follow-up for this principle will be...

» Their time frame for development will be...

When the summary is completed, invite the group to quiet themselves in preparation for your concluding prayer.

We give thanks, O God, for your guidance during this time of reflection and planning. May the work begun here, in your name, be continued in our community. May our goals, strategies, and practices lead to a community where faith—as strong as the woman's who touched Jesus' cloak—is infused in the lives and hearts of all.

And we pray, "Glory be to the Father..."

As we leave this holy space, let us offer one another a sign of peace.

Process Four: Full, Conscious, and Active Participation in Parish Life

Facilitator: At this gathering, we will prayerfully reflect on the principle of full, conscious, and active participation in parish life. First we will listen to words from sacred scripture and from *Our Hearts Were Burning Within Us*. Then, we will reflect individually for a few moments, followed by group discussion. Let us first quiet our minds and hearts and invite the Holy Spirit to guide our time together.

Generous God who begins the good work in us, we come to you as a community that seeks to be a place where all can participate. As we begin this process of reflection and planning, set our minds on your will, our hearts on your love, and our hands on your holy work. May your guidance help us to grow as a participatory community, one that invites all to the feast, and where all come to the feast. Amen.

Reflecting on Full Participation

A reading from the holy gospel according to Luke.

One of the dinner guests, on hearing this, said to him, "Blessed is anyone who will eat bread in the kingdom of God!" Then Jesus said to him, "Someone gave a great dinner and invited many. At the time for the dinner he sent his slave to say to those who had been invited, 'Come, for everything is ready now.' But they all alike began to make excuses. The first said to him, 'I have bought a piece of land, and I must go out and see it; please accept my regrets.' Another said, 'I have bought five yoke of oxen, and am going to try them out; please accept my regrets.' Another said, 'I have just been married, and therefore I cannot come.' So the slave returned and reported this to his master. Then the owner of the house became angry and said to his slave, 'Go out at once into the streets and lanes of the town and bring in the poor, the crippled, the blind, and the lame. And the slave said, 'Sir, what you ordered has been done, and there is still room.' Then the master said to the slave, 'Go out into the roads and lanes, and compel people to come in, so that my house may be filled. For I tell you, none of those who were invited will taste my dinner.'" ~LUKE 14:15–24

Our response to God's call to community "cannot remain abstract and unincarnated," but rather, "reveals itself concretely by a visible entry into a community of believers…a community which itself is a sign of transformation, a sign of newness of life: it is the Church, the visible sacrament of salvation." People find this community of faith in the parish and diocese, as well as in their families, small church communities, personal relationships, faith-based associations, and in the communion of saints of all times and places. Accordingly, faith formation helps adults make "a conscious and firm decision to live the gift and choice of faith through *membership in the Christian community,*" accepting "co-responsibility for the community's mission and internal life." Adults not only receive the ministries of the Christian community, they also contribute to its life and mission through the generous stewardship of their gifts. (*Our Hearts Were Burning Within Us,* p. 70–71)

Take a few moments to reflect on the words above, first silently as individuals, and then as a group.

What words or phrases strike you, particularly in light of your study of the principle of full, conscious, and active participation in parish life?

In a few sentences, summarize what you understand about such participation.

Questions to Guide Your Conversation

✦ What is our parish doing to enhance full participation

among all members? Are there ways for people to offer their ideas, discern ministries that could be of service within the parish or beyond it, or to offer their gifts as leaders? How does our parish embrace the mutual relationship of the Church needing the laity and the laity needing the Church?

✛ What practices are already in place that lead to full participation in the life of the parish? How can we build on these to grow as a fully participating community?

✛ Are there particular groups within the parish whose participation is minimized? What strategies could be developed to reach out to these groups in a special way?

✛ What new practices should we consider?

Following your discussion, summarize the consensus of the group with the statements below. These statements will be used to formulate your cohesive plan after all seven principles have been studied and discussed.

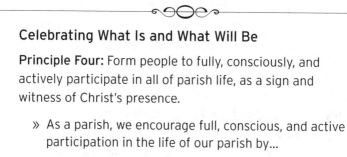

Celebrating What Is and What Will Be

Principle Four: Form people to fully, consciously, and actively participate in all of parish life, as a sign and witness of Christ's presence.

» As a parish, we encourage full, conscious, and active participation in the life of our parish by...

» As a result of our discussion we will explore these goals, strategies, or practices...

» The group that will be responsible for follow-up on this principle will be...

» Their time frame for development will be...

When the summary is completed, invite the group to quiet themselves in preparation for your concluding prayer.

We give thanks, O God, for your guidance during this time of reflection and planning. May the work begun here, in your name, be continued in our community. May our goals, strategies, and practices lead to a community in which there is full, active, and lively participation. May we all come to the feast in joy, with generous and thankful hearts.

And we pray, "Glory be to the Father..."

As we leave this holy space, let us offer one another a sign of peace.

Process Five: Discipleship and Stewardship

Facilitator: At this gathering, we will prayerfully reflect on the importance of living as disciples and stewards. First we will listen to words of sacred scripture and *Stewardship: A Disciple's Response.* Then, we will reflect individually for a few moments, followed by group discussion. Let us first quiet our minds and hearts and invite the Holy Spirit to guide our time together.

Generous God, who begins the good work in us, we come to you as a community that seeks to be disciples and stewards. As we begin this process of reflection and planning, set our minds on your will, our hearts on your love and our hands on your holy work. May your guidance help us to grow into willing disciples and generous stewards. Amen.

Reflecting on Discipleship and Stewardship

A reading from the holy gospel according to Matthew.

*After a long time the master of those slaves came and settled accounts with them. Then the one who had received the five talents came forward, bringing five more talents, saying, "Master, you handed over to me five talents; see, I have made five more talents." His master said to him, "Well done, good and trustworthy slave; you nave been trustworthy in a few things, I will put you in charge of many things; enter into the joy of your master." And the one with the two talents also came forward, saying, "Master, you handed over to me two talents; see, I have made two more talents." His master said to him, "Well done, good and trustworthy slave; you have been trustworthy in a few things, I will put you in charge of many things; enter into the joy of your master." Then the one who had received the one talent also came forward, saying, "Master, I knew that you were a harsh man, reaping where you did not sow, and gathering where you did not scatter seed; so I was afraid, and I went and hid your talent in the ground. Here you have what is yours." But his master replied, "You wicked and lazy slave! You knew, did you, that I reap where I did not sow, and gather where I did not scatter? Then you ought to have invested my money with the bankers, and on my return I would have received what was my own with interest. So take the talent from him, and give it to the one with the ten talents. For to all those who have, more will be given, and they will have an abundance; but from those who have nothing, even what they have will be taken away. As for this worthless slave, throw him into the outer darkness, where there will be weeping and gnashing of teeth." ~*MATTHEW 25:19–30

Mature disciples make a conscious, firm decision, carried out in action, to be followers of Jesus Christ no matter the cost to themselves. Beginning in conversion, change of mind and heart, this commitment is expressed not in a single action, or even in a number of actions over a period of time, but in an entire way of life. It means committing one's very self to the Lord. Stewardship is an expression of discipleship, with the power to change how we understand and live out our lives. Disciples who practice stewardship recognize God as the origin of life, the giver of freedom, the source of all they have and are and will be....They are grateful for what they have received and eager to cultivate their gifts out of love for God and one another. (*Stewardship: A Disciple's Response*, Introduction)

Take a few moments to reflect on the words above, first silently as individuals, and then as a group.

What words or phrases strike you, particularly in light of your study of the parish as the place where discipleship and stewardship are fostered?

In a few sentences, summarize what you understand about the parish as a place of living discipleship and stewardship.

Questions to Guide Your Reflection

✛ What is our parish doing to live the stewardship way of life? How do we connect evangelization, discipleship, and stewardship?

✛ What practices are already in place that lead to stewardship as a way of life, for people and for the parish community? How can we build on these to grow as disciples and stewards?

✛ Are there particular groups within the parish that are not formed as stewards or who are not invited and expected to grow as stewards over time? What strategies could be developed to reach out to those groups in a special way?

✛ What new practices should we consider?

Following your discussion, summarize the consensus of the group using the statements below. These statements will be used to formulate your cohesive plan after all seven principles have been studied and discussed.

Celebrate What Is and What Will Be

Principle Five: Challenge parishioners to live gospel values as disciples of Jesus Christ and as stewards of all they are, have, and will be.

» As a parish, we challenge people to live as disciples and stewards by...

» As a result of our discussion we will explore these goals, strategies, or practices...

» The group that will be responsible for follow-up on this principle will be...

» Their time frame for development will be...

When the summary is completed, invite the group to quiet themselves in preparation for your concluding prayer.

We give thanks, O God, for your guidance during this time of reflection and planning. May the work begun here in your name be continued in our community. May our goals, strategies, and practices lead to a community filled with generous hearts—of disciples and stewards who use their talents in a way pleasing to you and in service to your people.

And we pray, "Glory be to the Father..."

As we leave this holy space, let us offer one another a sign of peace.

PROCESS SIX: MEANINGFUL SERVICE

Facilitator: At this gathering, we will prayerfully reflect on the importance of living as disciples and stewards. First we will listen to the words from sacred scripture and *Go and Make Disciples.* Then, we will reflect individually for a few moments, followed by group discussion. Let us first quiet our minds and hearts, and invite the Holy Spirit to guide our time together.

Generous God, who begins the good work in us, we come to you as a community that seeks to be engaged in meaningful service. As we begin this process of reflection and planning, set our minds on your will, our hearts on your love, and our hands on your holy work. May your guidance help us to grow as a servant community, washing the feet of one another. Amen.

Reflecting on Meaningful Service

After he had washed their feet, had put on his robe, and had returned to the table, he said to them, "Do you know what I have done to you? You call me Teacher and Lord—and you are right, for that is what I am. So if I, your Lord and Teacher, have washed your feet, you also ought to wash one another's feet. For I have set you an example, that you also should do as I have done to you."
~JOHN 13:12–15

The fruits of evangelization are changed lives and a changed world—holiness and justice, spirituality, and peace. The validity of our having accepted the gospel does not only come from what we feel or what we know: it comes also from the way we serve others, especially the poorest, the most marginal, the most hurting, the most defenseless, and the least loved. An evangelization that stays inside ourselves is not an evangelization into the Good News of Jesus Christ. (*Go and Make Disciples,* p. 11)

Take a few moments to reflect on the words above, first silently as individuals, and then as a group.

What words or phrases strike you, particularly in light of your study of the importance of serving in the life of individuals and in the life of the community?

In a few sentences, summarize what you understand about the community being a people of meaningful service.

Questions to Guide Your Conversation

✛ What is our parish doing to encourage serving such as that described above?

✛ What practices are already in place that lead to opportunities for people to give or receive meaningful service, within the parish and beyond it? How can we build on these as we grow as a serving community?

✛ Are there particular groups within the parish that seem to need our service? Beyond the parish? What strategies could be developed to reach out to these groups in a special way?

✛ What new practices should we consider?

Following your discussion, summarize the consensus of the group with the statements below. These statements will be used to formulate your cohesive plan after all seven principles have been studied and discussed.

∞◠◯◠∞

Celebrating What Is and What Will Be

Principle Six: Become a parish in which every person is invited, encouraged, and expected to offer meaningful service within the parish and in their lives, and which acknowledges the ways in which ministry is given.

» As a parish, we help people to care for each other and for those in need by...

» As a result of our discussion we will explore these goals, strategies, or practices...

» The group that will be responsible for follow-up on this principle will be...

» Their time frame for development will be...

∞◠◯◠∞

When the summary is completed, invite the group to quiet themselves in preparation for your concluding prayer.

We give thanks, O God, for your guidance during this time of reflection and planning. May the work begun here, in your name, be continued in our community. May our goals, strategies and practices lead to a community of servants, willing to wash the feet of one another—within the parish and beyond its walls.

And we pray, "Glory be to the Father..."

As we leave this holy space, let us offer one another a sign of peace.

PROCESS SEVEN: CARING COMMUNITY

Facilitator: At this gathering, we will prayerfully reflect on the importance of caring in the life of our parish. First we will listen to the words from sacred scripture and the bishops' pastoral letter on stewardship. Then, we will reflect individually for a few moments, followed by group discussion. Let us first quiet our minds and hearts, and invite the Holy Spirit to guide our time together.

Generous God, who begins the good work in us, we come to you as a community that seeks to be caring and warm. As we begin this process of reflection and planning, set our minds on your will, our hearts on your love, and our hands on your holy work. May your guidance help us to grow as a caring community that lives and plays and worships together. Amen.

Reflecting on Caring

A reading from the Acts of the Apostles.

So those who welcomed his message were baptized, and that day about three thousand persons were added. They devoted themselves to the apostles' teaching and fellowship, to the breaking of bread and the prayers. Awe came upon everyone, because many wonders and signs were being done by the apostles. All who believed were together and had all things in common; they would sell their possessions and goods and distribute the proceeds to all, as any had need. Day by day, as they spent much time together in the temple, they broke bread at home and ate their food with glad and generous hearts, praising God and having the goodwill of all the people. And day by day the Lord added to their number those who were being saved. ~ACTS 2:42–47

As all this suggests, our individual lives as disciples and stewards must be seen in relation to God's larger purposes. From the outset of his covenanting, God had it in mind to make many one. He promised Abram: "I will make of you a great nation, and I will bless you; I will make your name great, so that you will be a blessing....All the communities of the earth shall find blessing in you" (Gn 12:2–3). In Jesus, the kingdom of God is inaugurated—a kingdom open to all. Those who enter into Jesus' New Covenant find themselves growing in a union of minds and hearts with others who also have responded to God's call. They find their hearts and minds expanding to embrace all men and women, especially those in need, in a communion of mercy and love. (*Stewardship, A Disciple's Response*, p. 37)

Take a few moments to reflect on the words above, first silently as individuals, and then as a group.

What words or phrases strike you, particularly in light of your study of the importance of caring in the life of individuals and in the life of the community?

In a few sentences, summarize what you understand about the community being a people of care.

Questions to Guide Your Conversation

✛ What is our parish doing to encourage caring such as that described above? In what ways does our parish support the formation of communities? How are people engaged in the four simple experiences described in the Acts of the Apostles?

✛ What practices are already in place that lead to caring among parishioners and flowing out from the community for those in need? How can we build on these as we grow as a caring community?

✢ Are there particular groups within the parish that seem to need our care? Beyond the parish? What strategies could be developed to reach out to those groups in a special way?

✢ What new practices should we consider?

Following your discussion, summarize the consensus of the group using the statements below. These statements will be used to formulate your cohesive plan after all seven principles have been studied and discussed.

Celebrating What Is and What Will Be

Principle Seven: Create a community in which parishioners care for one another and for those in need in the community and the world.

» As a parish, we help people to care for each other and for those in need by...

» As a result of our discussion we will explore these goals, strategies, or practices...

» The group that will be responsible for follow-up on this principle will be...

» Their time frame for development will be...

When the summary is completed, invite the group to quiet themselves in preparation for your concluding prayer.

We give thanks, O God, for your guidance during this time of reflection and planning. May the work begun here, in your name, be continued in our community. May our goals, strategies, and practices lead to a caring, loving, and spirit-filled community, a place through whom you bring others to you "day by day."

And we pray, "Glory be to the Father..."

As we leave this holy space, let us offer one another a sign of peace.

Conclusion

Just as we have mapped out and shared the principles, vision, and practices of stewardship in this book, we have also done so in workshops, professional discussions, and conversations with people of ministry throughout the United States. Inevitably, two questions arise. How do you *do* all this? Or, how do you *pay* for all this? Both questions, ultimately, are answered by stewardship.

Changes will begin to happen as your parish embraces stewardship more fully. The first shift will come when the call for ministries and the people who wish to be involved in ministries are greater than can be coordinated by the pastor or pastoral staff. Your initial reaction may be to stop the development out of fear that things will get out of control. This is the point when you do need to slow things down, just long enough to draw people together to discern what is really needed by your parishioners and those you serve. This isn't about *doing* more necessarily, but of having a clear vision, and then finding ways to live that vision in every dimension of parish life.

ENTRUSTING AND EQUIPPING

Another shift will happen gradually, if you guide your parish in a way that will foster the transition, when those in leadership learn to *entrust* and *equip* others to be meaningfully involved as coordinators and leaders. There are skills you will have to acquire as you make this shift, since most of us are trained (or have learned through experience) to *do* the work of ministry rather than to *equip* others to be partners with us in this. You will have to help people discern who the appropriate parishioners are for leadership or coordinating roles, develop structures of communication (some of those are described above) and provide training for them. Once ministries begin to function in this way, however, it is freeing for current leaders, who can now keep the bigger picture of the vision you hold in common and ministry needs and practices in mind. The parishioners who are entrusted with ministry will find themselves able to draw others into service with them. The ministries multiply, simply and gracefully.

How do we pay for it all? The truth is, the more engaged parishioners are, and the more fully they grow as stewards, the less we have to worry about funding the ministry within or beyond our parish. Remember the pastor at the beginning of the book? He said that it would be wonderful if, in the process of people growing closer to Christ, the bills were paid! Folks in stewardship parishes throughout the U.S. will tell you that's exactly what happens, and in ways we would never have imagined. Trusting in the Holy Spirit and discerning where and how you as a parish are called to act are the true marks of the steward, as individuals and as a parish community. Just as our families learn to take leaps of faith occasionally as they commit themselves more deeply as stewards, sometimes the parish family must do the same. Simply remember the words of the letter to the Ephesians: "glory be to him whose power working in us can do infinitely more than we can ask or imagine!" (3:20).

DO YOU HAVE THE VISION?

Do you have the vision? Are you ready to act on all you have read and considered? Are you ready to become a parish filled with disciples and stewards with generous hearts that mirror the heart of Christ? Perhaps your parish is already on this journey of discipleship and you were looking for a few thoughts to encourage you or to give you hope. Are you now prepared to share the ideas you have found yourself contemplating with others? How will you begin or continue to employ the seven principles of parish life as your community grows as a family of faith? If you are ready to share the vision with others, draw together other leaders to study, discuss, and plan accordingly. It is time to take your next step, to become the people envisioned at the end of *Stewardship: A Disciple's Response*:

> In light of all of this, it only remains for all of us to ask ourselves this question: Do we also wish to be disciples of Jesus Christ? The Spirit is ready to show us the way— a way of which stewardship is a part. Genesis, telling the story of creation, says God looked upon what had been made and found it good; and seeing the world's goodness, God entrusted it to human beings. "The Lord God planted a garden" and placed there human persons "to cultivate and care for it" (Gn 2:8, 15).

Now, as then and always, it is a central part of the human vocation that we be good stewards of what we have received—this garden, this divine/human workshop, this world and all that is in it—setting our minds and hearts and hands to the task of creating and redeeming in cooperation with our God, Creator and Lord of all.

Helpful Resources

The resources listed below have been particularly helpful to many parishes in the formation of leaders and the preparation of strategies and practices such as the ones described in this book. A more complete description of the resource, additional titles, ordering information, and helpful links are available on our Web site: www.thegenerousheart.com.

Conway, Daniel, *What Do I Own and What Owns Me? A Spirituality of Stewardship*, Twenty-Third Publications, 2005

Kollar, Judith Ann, *A User-Friendly Parish: Becoming a More Welcoming Community*, Twenty-Third Publications, 2001

Smith, Colleen, *Sharing God's Gifts*, Our Sunday Visitor, 2001

Hueckel, Sharon, *Stewardship by the Book: Scriptural Quotations on Stewardship*, OSV Pastoral Ministry Series, 1996

International Catholic Stewardship Council, Inc., *Stewardship: Disciples Respond, A Practical Guide for Pastoral Leaders*, 1997

Mahan, Daniel J., *More Than Silver or Gold: Homilies of a Stewardship Priest*, Saint Catherine of Siena Press, 2005.

U.S. Catholic Bishops, *Stewardship, A Disciple's Response*, Tenth Anniversary Edition, USCCB, 2002

Winseman, Dr. Albert, *Growing Engaged Churches*, Gallup Press, 2007

Winseman, Dr. Albert, *Living Your Strengths*, Catholic Edition, Gallup Press, 2006

ORGANIZATIONS OF PARTICULAR INTEREST

The mission of the International Catholic Stewardship Council is to foster an environment in which stewardship is understood, accepted, and practiced throughout the Catholic Church. The ICSC holds annual conferences and other leader development events, publishes stewardship materials, and provides networking opportunities for parish and diocesan stewardship leaders.

The work of the Gallup Organization has been cited throughout this book. In addition to the two publications listed above, Gallup has developed a brief survey parishes can administer to measure parishioner engagement and spiritual commitment. The ME25 survey is based on the research briefly described in this volume and more extensively in *Growing Engaged Churches*. Additionally, Gallup provides leader training in engagement and strengths development for ministry professionals at their national headquarters in Omaha, Nebraska and at regional gatherings throughout the United States.